pregnancy
journal

*A Week-by-Week Guide to a Happy,
Healthy Pregnancy*

Paula Spencer Scott

Illustrated by Margaret Rubiano

PETER PAUPER PRESS, INC.
White Plains, New York

Acknowledgments

Juanita Covert superbly supplied essential research and legwork for the preparation of this manuscript, as well as shared I've-just-been-there insights, having recently delivered her first child, Isabella.

PETER PAUPER PRESS
Fine Books and Gifts Since 1928

OUR COMPANY

In 1928, at the age of twenty-two, Peter Beilenson began printing books on a small press in the basement of his parents' home in Larchmont, New York. Peter—and later his wife, Edna—sought to create fine books that sold at "prices even a pauper could afford."

Today, still family owned and operated, Peter Pauper Press continues to honor our founders' legacy—and our customers' expectations—of beauty, quality, and value.

Designed by Heather Zschock

Illustrations by Margaret Rubiano

Copyright © 2012
Peter Pauper Press, Inc.
202 Mamaroneck Avenue
White Plains, NY 10601
All rights reserved
ISBN 978-1-4413-0982-2
Printed in China
7 6 5 4 3 2 1

Visit us at www.peterpauper.com

✳ C O N T E N T S ✳

Introduction

Your Incredible Journey

Welcome to an amazing, surprising, strange, thrilling, and topsy-turvy season of your life—nine months like no others.

Yes, that's a broad range of adjectives to link with pregnancy. It's impossible to limit a description of an experience like having a baby to just a word or two.

Enter this journal.

Because the journey from newly pregnant woman to full-fledged mother is filled with so much, it's helpful to have a special place to store your discoveries and your memories. Although no two pregnancies are alike, there's plenty of common ground in terms of topics you're apt to encounter. Ahead are great highs (like the first time you feel your baby move within you) as well as a few lows (like when nausea or a backache leaves you feeling a bit less glowy than the whole world seems to expect you to feel). And lots of wonders in between.

What you'll find here:

AN OUTLET. Use this journal as a place of refuge where you can write down the details of your incredible journey. Celebrate. Vent. Absorb. Mull. Marvel. Scribble lists or compose perfect sentences—whatever works for you. In addition to lots of writing space, we'll provide some "food for thought" prompts along the way.

A RECORD. To whom did you first break the news? When did you buy your first maternity top? What tests did you have, and when? Which names did you consider? Jot key details like these down for a permanent memento of your pregnancy story.

A KEEPSAKE-FOLDER. Use the inside back cover pocket to store such keepsakes as ultrasound photos, doctor's notes, and nursery ideas.

A COMPANION. In these pages you'll find helpful tips, insightful facts, fun ideas, and loads of empathy to smooth your progress from week to week.

A PREGNANCY GUIDE. Time-targeted, reliable information addresses your specific concerns along the way. We give an overview of the highlights that characterize each of the three trimesters of pregnancy, as well as a summary of dos and don'ts.

A WEEKLY SUPPORT SYSTEM. Then, for each week, we offer information about three different dimensions of pregnancy:

	BABY UPDATE. How's he or she growing? What's happening in your womb this week?
	BODY UPDATE. Advice and comfort tips on the physical side of being pregnant.
	MIND UPDATE. Insights about possible mental, emotional, or spiritual issues.

AN INSPIRATION. Quotations about pregnancy and motherhood sprinkled throughout these pages remind you that you're not alone—you're joining a league of mothers as old as, well, (wo)mankind itself.

*Here's wishing you a healthy pregnancy,
and happy journaling along the way.*

GREAT EXPECTATIONS!

On being pregnant:

FIRSTS

First person I told the news to (describe)

The first person I told was Anthony I called him at the doctors when they told me the news and told him we are having a baby

When I first felt pregnant (and in what way)

First doctor visit

First heard the baby's heartbeat *October 9, 2012*

When I first wore maternity clothes

First felt the baby move

Other firsts

I was overwhelmed by emotion when I found out I was pregnant. My husband and I had been trying to get pregnant for a long time. I showed my husband the ultrasound image, and our eyes filled with tears. We could not speak for several moments.

JENNIFER GARRETT

WEIGHTS AND MEASUREMENTS

Pre-pregnancy weight:

WEEK	WEIGHT	WAIST
4		
6		
8		
10		
12		
14		
16		
18		
20		
22		
24		
26		
28		
30		
32		
34		
36		
37		
38		
39		
40		

TESTS AND RESULTS

TEST	DATE	RESULT

Your First Trimester

(CONCEPTION TO 12 WEEKS)

Off to a Great Start

All of pregnancy is a transition—but the first trimester feels especially so. These first weeks are all about getting used to the idea of being pregnant and doing what you can to safeguard the well-being of the new life you're carrying.

At first, it might not seem like much is happening; doubt, anxiety, or impatience sometimes race ahead of concrete physical signs. Then come the symptoms, catching up to your initial thoughts and, often, overtaking them. In a few brief weeks, you travel from the unreality of your big news to feeling that the pregnancy is unmistakably real.

One of the best predictors of a healthy baby is a healthy mother. Do what's in your power to give your baby a great head start. Now's a terrific time to shore up (or fine-tune) your health habits. What you eat or drink can affect your baby. So how you spend your day—exercise, the kind of substances you handle, your stress level, and the amount of rest and relaxation you get—can influence the health of both of you.

Ideally, doctors like women to have a preconception exam, before pregnancy begins. This allows you to get preexisting medical conditions under control, and to have tests (such as a Pap smear, a mammogram, or a blood pressure reading) to rule out other possible obstacles to a successful pregnancy. But don't worry if you've conceived before such a medical exam. There's still plenty of time to begin great prenatal care and to take care of yourself and your baby.

The first trimester is a time of getting things going: your health habits, your medical care, your support network, your idea of yourself as a pregnant woman. It's a lot to absorb. Luckily, pregnancy progresses slowly and steadily, giving you time to make the mental and practical life adjustments you need.

First Trimester Dos and Don'ts

Do...

- Make an appointment with an ob-gyn, midwife, or family doctor as soon as a home pregnancy test confirms the news. The earlier you start receiving prenatal care, the better for you and your baby. You can expect to have a history taken, receive initial screenings and tests, get a prescription for prenatal vitamins, and (the best part) get an official due date!

- Take your prescribed prenatal vitamins daily, if you can. For some women, the added iron makes early nausea worse. *Tip:* Try taking the vitamin on a full stomach.

- Start making shifts toward a healthier, well-balanced diet as soon as you know you are pregnant, if you haven't already. You probably know the drill: Switch from white breads, pasta, and rice to whole grains. Eliminate trans fats and substitute healthier fats. Choose lean proteins (white meats, fish, eggs, low-fat dairy) and promise yourself to choose more fruits and vegetables every day. The U.S. Food and Drug Administration advises pregnant women to avoid shark, swordfish, king mackerel, and tilefish because of mercury levels, and to limit consumption of other fish to about 12 ounces per week (which is about three servings).

- Target nutrients you especially need now. They include:

  Iron. Necessary for hemoglobin in the blood. Found in dried fruits, grains, legumes, and dark leafy vegetables.

  Folate. Helps prevent neural tube defects. Your prenatal vitamin contains it, but it's also found in bread, cereal, and pasta (which are fortified according to U.S. government requirements), as well as legumes, soy, brewer's yeast, and dark leafy veggies.

  Calcium. Builds fetal teeth and bones without depleting your reserves. Low-fat yogurt or milk, dark leafy greens, and salmon are sources.

  Zinc. Helps fetal growth. Found in fish, eggs, milk, and wheat germ.

- Keep moving. Run your current exercise routine by your doctor. It's now thought that most activities, other than scuba diving or sports with a high risk of falls, can be safely continued in the first trimester. The benefits to mood, baby, energy level, and overall well-being are tremendous! If you've never bothered much with workouts before but feel motivated now, good for you. Walking, moderate swimming, and prenatal yoga are all perfect forms of exercise for pregnancy because you can continue them throughout your term.

- Schedule X-rays after the first trimester, if possible.

- Stay away from insecticides and fungicides, harsh chemicals, aerosols, and lead (in some paints and pipes). Other potentially dangerous substances include rubber cement, stains, finishes, and varnish and paint removers. Some doctors also recommend postponing hair dyes and perms until after the first trimester.

- Enjoy couple time. Enjoy favorite pastimes together and remember that this big change can seem all the more unreal to your mate, who, unlike you, doesn't "feel" any different.

- Dream a little. Don't get so caught up in the medical advice and planning that you neglect to begin to imagine your future baby and your new family.

Don't...

- Smoke or spend time around people who are smoking.

- Drink alcohol. Although there's been lots of debate about how much is too much, most experts advise erring on the side of complete abstinence. Even "near beers" and nonalcoholic wines can contain some alcohol (unless they specify "alcohol-free").

- Use other known damaging substances. These include: marijuana and other illegal drugs; tanning booths; douches.

- Heat it up. Skip hot tubs, whirlpools, or Jacuzzis during pregnancy, as it's not a good idea to become overheated. Some doctors even nix electric blankets and long, hot soaks in the bath.

- Handle or eat raw meat, raw seafood, or raw eggs, to avoid bacteria and parasites. Also skip sushi and sashimi; rare hamburgers or steaks; unpasteurized milk or juice; Caesar salad dressing or certain ice creams that contain raw eggs; soft cheeses such as feta, brie, Camembert, and queso blanco. (Cottage cheese and cream cheese are fine.)

- Change cat litter. Recruit someone else to do the job, since handling cat feces raises your risk of contracting the parasite that causes the infection toxoplasmosis. Also wash your hands after handling a cat, and keep cats off tables and countertops.

More Don'ts...

- **Be blithe about vitamins, supplements, and herbals.** Once you know you're pregnant, even before your first prenatal exam, call your doctor to run through any prescriptions you now take. Certain acne medications, for example, such as Accutane and Retin-A, can harm a developing fetus. Nor should you assume that a "natural" pregnancy is necessarily a safe one. Botanical products are not government regulated and are often untested. That's why it's wise to run anything—including over-the-counter meds and holistic remedies advertised as safe for pregnancy—by your primary caregiver.

- **"Eat for two."** Your caloric needs barely rise in the first trimester—about the equivalent of an extra glass of milk. Most women need to gain only 3 to 4 pounds (1.36 to 1.81 kg) in the first trimester.

- **Go overboard on the baby gear.** Give yourself this trimester to get a firm grounding on what's happening in your life first. You have weeks ahead to ogle and splurge!

- **Obsess too much.** Women have been having babies forever. The occasional dietary slip-up or whiff of a passerby's cigar won't harm your baby. Remember that being relaxed is more useful to your well-being than over-worry.

Conception

Meet Your New Zygote!

After sperm and egg unite, the egg closes its doors (in the form of its outer membrane) to other potential suitors. The precious baby you'll get to meet face-to-face in nine months has begun life as a zygote, a fertilized egg. It then multiplies into a tiny bunch of cells (about the size of the head of a pin), and is called a *blastocyst*. Within 3 or 4 days, this blastocyst burrows into the lining of your uterus so it can receive oxygen and nutrients and discard waste through your bloodstream. Its cells are also multiplying rapidly right now. By week 3, amniotic fluid (the "water" in "I think my water broke!"), which serves to cushion, warm, and protect your baby in the amniotic sac, has begun to surround it.

When's Your Due Date?

Pregnancy lasts about 38 weeks from conception to birth, or 40 weeks from the last menstrual period (LMP) to birth. To calculate your estimated due date, add 9 months and 7 days (a total of 280 days) to your LMP date.

Remember, though, that this due date is an *estimate* based on the average pregnancy. Most women (80 percent) give birth within 2 weeks of their due date—2 weeks before or 2 weeks after—but only about 4 to 5 percent deliver on their actual due date. As your pregnancy progresses, measurements of your uterus (fundus height), ultrasounds, and other physical observations will reinforce this due date and help your doctor assess the progress of your pregnancy.

I learned i was pregnant at the doctors. They were doing a procedure and had to test to see if i was pregnant and when they said i was i was filled with joy and very excited to bring a child into this world.

Questions for my health professional

When I learned I was pregnant, I felt delighted, proud.
Like I had a secret that I had to keep.

KATHY HAYDEN

THE COUNTDOWN BEGINS
Week 4

 ## Baby Update: SMALL MATTERS

By now, the blastocyst has divided into an embryo and a placenta. The embryo, which is your baby-to-be, is tinier than a grain of rice, with two distinct layers—the *epiblast* and *hypoblast*. As it grows, its cells will differentiate into specific jobs—the foundations for blood, nerves, and organs, for example.

The placenta is a very cool support system. This organ emerges to help produce hormones and to connect to the blood vessels in your uterine lining—all so it can, eventually, transfer oxygen and nutrients to your baby and discard released waste.

 ## Body Update: FIRST SIGNS OF PREGNANCY

Many women notice changes in their breasts even before they miss a period. Your breasts may feel tender or larger, and the area around your nipples (areola) may look darker, larger, and/or bumpier. Breasts may tingle or feel more sensitive.

Sudden fatigue is another big clue. It can range from just-noticeable tiredness to flat-out exhaustion. You may begin feeling nauseated or bloated. Lots of women mistake these early symptoms for a case of the flu. Also common: A sudden aversion to smells or tastes that you never reacted to before (such as meat frying or chocolate). You may also feel the need to urinate more often.

Being "late" of course is the big bell-ringer. Some women will still see a little spotting, staining, or yellowish discharge around the time their period would be due.

False negatives are more common than false positives with home pregnancy tests. That's why, if you suspect you're pregnant, it's a good idea to wait a few days and re-test. Levels of the hormone hCG *(human chorionic gonadotropin)*, produced by the pregnancy and detected by a pregnancy test, double every day in early pregnancy.

Mind Update: FIRST REACTIONS

Excited? Scared? Nervous? Ambivalent? Or are you still in a state of disbelief? All of these are perfectly natural first reactions to discovering that you are pregnant. There's no one "right" way to be. Give yourself a little time to absorb the news at the pace and way that feels right to you.

Don't be surprised if the way you feel isn't at all like what you expected. Maybe you tried so many months to get pregnant, and anticipated this big moment for so long, that its actuality is a bit of a letdown (especially if you're not feeling so hot). Maybe pregnancy caught you by surprise and you and your partner have mismatched reactions.

Many new mothers-to-be are so absorbed by their initial reactions to pregnancy—how they feel, what it means to their life, work, relationship, and plans—that they aren't even able to focus on the baby yet. Yup, that's normal too. Your becoming a mother is every bit as seismic as your having a baby. And while the two go hand-in-hand (obviously!), they're slightly different realities. Luckily you have ample time to get used to both.

Dating Your Pregnancy

A word about how this journal counts the weeks: The way that most doctors date a pregnancy, used here, is by *gestational age*, also called *menstrual age*. This means that the first official day of your pregnancy term is the first day of your last menstrual period (LMP). Conception usually occurs around two weeks after your LMP. So when you are "13 weeks pregnant," or in week 13 of this book, you have technically been pregnant for 11 weeks. Some doctors still use *fertilization age* (also called *fetal age* or *ovulatory age*, marking a pregnancy from the date you conceived), but since fertilization can be hard to pinpoint, dating by gestational age is considered more accurate.

How am I feeling?

I am always tired & have morning sickness. Its exciting to see my stomache start to get bigger.

Although I wanted to be pregnant, I knew that the following months would be an unpredictable adventure!

MELISSA LIPPINCOTT

Musings and photos

Week 5

Baby Update

Your little embryo—that's what it's now called—is going through momentous changes. The embryo consists of three layers: *ectoderm*, *endoderm*, and *mesoderm*. As befits their sci-fi names, each has a futuristic job to do. The ectoderm will develop into the brain and nervous system, skin, hair, nails, tooth enamel, and mammary and sweat glands. The endoderm will develop into the lungs, gastrointestinal tract, pancreas, thyroid, and liver. And the mesoderm will become the heart and circulatory system, skeleton, blood system, urogenital system, and the muscles and connective tissues.

Already this week, your baby's heart begins to beat regularly; arm and leg buds appear; and the eyes, ears, and skeleton begin to form. The placenta and umbilical cord begin to function around this time, too.

Body Update: THE ART OF LISTENING TO YOUR BODY

When you're really tired, do you nap, or at least put your feet up? When your stomach is full, do you stop eating? These are common examples of listening to your body. That's a really important skill during pregnancy, because your trusty, hardworking body has a lot to tell you. The changes that every system within you will experience in the coming months are tremendous. If you try to plow on ahead as if there's "nothing different," you're denying reality, and that's never an optimal way to live.

Try to make the commitment to slow down a little bit and hear what your body wants to say. Its aches and pains might be telling you to ease up on certain activities, to stretch or have a massage, or to sleep in a different position. If certain smells or tastes are suddenly objectionable, avoid them. (It's no coincidence that many women report disliking the smell of cigarettes or the taste of alcohol in pregnancy, both things that are known to negatively affect a growing fetus.)

Your body will tell you what it likes, too! You might find yourself calmed and soothed by sitting quietly and rubbing your belly, for example. A morning walk might pep you up and quell nausea all day long. The advice of doctors and pregnancy guidebooks boils down to suggestions that have been shown to work for most women. But only you have your body, and only you can hear what it wants most from you.

Mind Update: SPREADING THE NEWS, MAYBE

Whom will you tell that you're pregnant, and when? Deciding can involve a series of very personal choices. Some new parents are inclined to share their happy news with the world (or, at least, everyone they know) as soon as the home pregnancy test confirms it. Others prefer to keep mum for a while. They may simply want to keep this very special secret between themselves for a few precious weeks, or prefer to wait until the greatest danger of miscarriage is past, usually between 9 and 12 weeks.

Some newly expectant mothers compromise. They confide in a close friend, sister, or their own mother, to have someone with whom they can talk or compare notes (besides their partner). Then they wait a bit longer to tell other friends and family members, colleagues, and casual acquaintances.

Think, too, about how you will make your announcements. In a series of elated phone calls? At a big "surprise" party? Different audiences might warrant different approaches. Some mothers have been known to frame pictures of their first ultrasound to present to unsuspecting grandparents-to-be. At work, you might want to have a confidential talk with your human resources representative first, to discuss options about maternity leave and benefits, so that you can better formulate a plan to present to your supervisor when you tell her.

What's happening—inside and out?

Pregnancy, emotionally, is like turmoil at various stages, while the reality sinks in.
And it never really does until the baby arrives.

MARTHA ZSCHOCK

Week 6

 ## Baby Update

This week your speck of a baby is hardly 1/4-inch (0.6 cm) long—picture a dried pea in the shape of a curled tadpole. (The measurement of your baby's length is now calculated from the crown of the head to the buttocks because the legs are curled close to the chest.) Arms and legs are becoming longer and they now grow hand and feet buds, with tiny, webbed fingers and toes. Your baby's jaw, tongue, nose, and lungs also begin to form. Muscle fibers are starting to grow, and your baby's intestines and brain continue to develop.

It's possible to actually hear your baby's busy heartbeat (going much faster than your own—about 100 to 130 beats per minute) with a vaginal ultrasound. It's working hard to circulate blood to support all this rapid growth.

 ## Body Update: EASING EARLY DISCOMFORTS

Hollywood's favorite pregnancy ailments are morning sickness and fainting (which is actually pretty rare), but you're probably feeling other discomforts, too. Luckily, there are things you can do to feel better.

IF you suffer from gas, bloating, and heartburn: Avoid gaseous, fried, and fatty foods. Eat slowly. A leisurely walk after a meal—even if it's just around your house—can also help.

IF your breasts feel swollen and sore: Try a new bra that fits better and gives you more support. You may need several bra updates during your pregnancy, so err on the side of roominess when you choose one. Avoid underwires, which can pinch or even compress mammary glands. Some women are helped by wearing a bra to sleep.

IF you're getting headaches: Try nonmedical treatments first, such as fresh air, rest, or a relaxation technique. Acetaminophen (at recommended dosage and frequency) is safe, but it's best to avoid aspirin, ibuprofen, and other medications without medical approval. If headaches are persistent or severe, tell your doctor.

IF increased vaginal discharge bothers you: Try wearing a panty liner and changing it often. Cotton underwear tends to be more comfortable than synthetic.

IF you're congested (an unexpected but common side effect of pregnancy): Try using a humidifier and elevating your head when you sleep. Also remember to drink lots of fluids. Don't take antihistamines or other cold medications without your doctor's okay.

Mind Update: EXPECTING CHANGE

"Your life will never be the same." Heard that yet? Don't let it unnerve you. As ominous as the sentiment might sound, it's based in truth—here's why it really will be okay.

It's true a baby will likely keep you from some enjoyable activities you're used to, especially the first few months. You may be so distracted by your new priorities, however, that you don't miss the activities as much as you might have expected. Once you "pay your dues" taking care of a newborn, you can begin to bring some of those activities back. Plus you get to spend time playing, cuddling, and finding joy in unexpected ways.

Sleep deprivation is not a myth. Your newborn will need you constantly, at all hours of the day and night, for food, soothing, diaper changes, and even help getting to sleep. But take comfort knowing that the more you respond to your baby's needs, the more he learns to trust and love you. What seems like thankless hours, early on, are actually setting the stage for all his future emotions and learning. And once he starts smiling (around six weeks), it all seems so much easier!

Even though much of your day will be dedicated to taking care of your baby, there are ways to make time for yourself and other relationships. You and your partner will get to see and admire whole new sides of each other, too. So yes, big changes are ahead, but, on balance, the gains will likely be more plentiful than the losses.

DID YOU KNOW that you may be referred to as an "elderly primigravida" if you are only in your 30s? It simply means you are an "older" (in obstetrical terms) first-time mother.

Musings

Likes and dislikes

What I'm craving this week

pickles
Chocolate

Smells and tastes that bug me

burgers
Chinese food

Being pregnant gives you a whole new appreciation for your mother.

BARBARA PAULDING

Week 7

Baby Update

Your embryo is still tiny but—ta da!—reaches the size of a small berry, about half an inch (1.3 cm). Her head is clearly oversized and her skin very thin—but don't let this awkward, delicate appearance fool you. Strong growth is unmistakable. She can already move in the amniotic sac. Fingers and toes are separating, and elbows are now visible. Vital organs are developing, as well as fine details: teeth, eyelids, nipples, and hair follicles. The liver is now producing red blood cells, and blood vessels in the umbilical cord represent your baby's lifeline—carrying oxygen and nutrients between the two of you.

Body Update: NAUSEA HELPERS

Morning sickness peaks from weeks 7 to 12, generally—but its timing and severity vary considerably from woman to woman. Morning sickness is the most deceptive misnomer of pregnancy. You can feel sick to your stomach any time of the day, or even all day. Symptoms do tend to be worst first thing in the morning for many women.

Nobody knows exactly what causes nausea and vomiting, or why symptoms can be so different from one woman to another. (Up to 90 percent of women experience some degree of it.) Hormonal changes are almost certainly a trigger, and discomfort eases, in all but a small percentage of cases, by the end of the first trimester.

Some tactics that can help in the meantime:

- **Eat strategically.** Don't avoid food completely when nausea strikes because this can actually make you feel worse. Try small, light meals, and keep a stash of light snacks such as crackers and fruits (or other foods that appeal) on hand for nibbling. If you eat a little before you feel really hungry, you may be able to stave off an attack. Avoid heavily sauced foods, junk food, or greasy items as they're slow to digest.

- **Stay vertical.** Lying down immediately or soon after eating can make you queasy. Snack when you wake up in the morning, before getting out of bed. If you can, stay in bed sitting upright for about 15 minutes before getting up. Snack again before you go to bed.

- **Drink lots of water and other fluids.** Dehydration can exacerbate nausea.

- **Give your nose a break.** Avoid stuffy rooms by keeping windows open. Because strong smells can trigger nausea, remove highly scented soaps, perfumes, and foods from your home.

- **Try ginger.** Most so-called "pregnancy teas" and botanical tonics are suspect in pregnancy because they are unregulated and untested, and can cause serious side effects including miscarriage. Exception: A cup or two of ordinary ginger tea. (It's sold in many groceries, or you can grate a little fresh ginger in hot water.) Ginger has been shown to calm queasiness.

- **Try acupressure bands.** Sold over-the-counter, these wristbands have a plastic disc that rests on your pressure point. They're advertised for motion sickness and seasickness, but seem to be a low-tech remedy for pregnancy sickness as well.

- **Consult with your doctor if you vomit more than twice a day, can't keep anything down at all, or seem to be dropping weight quickly.** A small percentage of women suffer especially severe morning sickness (called hyperemesis gravidarum, or HG), which warrants close supervision in order to avoid dehydration and other problems. Vitamin B6 has been found to ease symptoms; your doctor can recommend a dosage.

Mind Update: REMEMBER WHEN... ?

It's hard to believe, but nine months from now your pregnancy will probably become a blur. In addition to your journal, consider preserving some of your memories of this special time. Your family will love looking back. Some ideas:

Write a letter to your baby. Tell your baby how you feel about meeting and getting to know him and what you look forward to doing with him. Share your hopes and dreams for him. Ask your partner to write something, too. Reading each other's letters has the added benefit of giving one another insights into your feelings now.

Track your changing shape. Choose a particular day of the month and have someone photograph you. (Profiles are especially dramatic.) Take snapshots of your baby preparations too, like decorating the nursery. It's a good idea to start a scrapbook or photo album now, since you'll have little time to get organized after the baby is born.

Start a memory box. Use a decorative photo storage box or the inside back cover pocket of this book to keep mementos as you go: ultrasound printouts, doctors' notes, nursery decor ideas ripped out of magazines, a copy of the e-mail you sent to your best friend to share the good news.

A letter to my baby ...

When I listen to my body, it says …

Everything changes. Your body is in control and tells you
when and what to eat, where and when to sleep.

DONNA KILMER

Week 8

Baby Update

Not yet an inch (2.5 cm) long, your baby is taking on a more familiar human shape. The body straightens out a bit and the head becomes more erect. The embryonic "tail" is receding (it will eventually be the tailbone). The limbs, fingers, and toes are getting longer and, interestingly, the hands reach for each other over the heart. Facial features are becoming more distinct, too, and nerve cells in your baby's brain are making important connections.

Body Update: VITAMINS AND SUPPLEMENTS

Your baby depends on you for nutrients, vitamins, and minerals vital to growth and development. For this reason, your doctor has probably recommended a special prenatal vitamin at your first office visit. Remember to take it daily. Reinforce the habit by doing this at the same time each day, such as after breakfast. That timing has the added advantage of lessening the likelihood of nausea, since you'll have something in your stomach. Taking your vitamin with orange juice helps your body better absorb the iron in it.

Taking a daily prenatal vitamin doesn't excuse you from seeking out good nutrition from the foods you eat. Vitamins and minerals are most readily absorbed in their natural form. Nor do prenatal supplements include the full recommended allowance of certain nutrients, such as protein, calcium, or iron.

You do need to be careful with vitamins, though. Don't take two doses in one day to "catch up" if you miss a day, for example. Certain vitamins, such as vitamin A, can be dangerous in amounts over the recommended daily allowance (more than 10,000 IU of vitamin A is toxic). There are cases where your doctor might suggest a supplement, such as added iron in the event of anemia, or extra calcium. Follow medical advice in this area rather than self-treating.

Mind Update: HOW TO GET THE MOST OUT OF CHECKUPS

How do you like your care provider so far? It's important to have a good relationship to feel most comfortable and informed. You'll also be able to receive more personalized care if you like and respect one another. If you are not on the same page philosophically, or just don't mesh, better to make a change at this point in your pregnancy.

Some ways to make your appointments better:

- Keep a list of questions and concerns in a handy place, such as in your date book, on your refrigerator, or in this journal. Then you won't forget them. Bring the list to your appointment. This makes you look proactive, not obsessive.

- Ask questions, no matter how foolish or gross they may seem. Your care provider may have heard everything before, but you haven't, and that's what matters.

- Clarify anything you don't completely understand. It often helps to repeat what your doctor tells you in your own words to make sure you've got it right.

- Double check with your doctor what you read or hear about pregnancy if you want to be sure about something. Don't just take your mother's word for it.

- Prod your doctor further if something she's said doesn't seem right to you. Remember you're a team, and your own instincts are useful guides.

- Take a notebook with you and take notes during your doctor visits.

- Make small talk. Sometimes seemingly unimportant observations or comments you make can trigger your doctor to tell you useful information.

- Accept handouts. Pick up brochures on pregnancy. Written information that you can read over at your leisure may clarify points made during appointments.

- Be honest, open, and specific when you describe how you feel. Here is one place where you should definitely drop the "happy mask" and be candid. Your well-being, and your baby's, depends on it.

DID YOU KNOW that it's common for your clothes to feel tight in the waist weeks before you actually "show"?

My emotional weather report

*It was difficult to comprehend how the fertilized egg in my
uterus was going to grow into a person.*

RAEANNE SARAZEN

Musings and photos

Week 9

 ## Baby Update

Your baby is now about 1 to 1-1/4 inches (2.5 to 3.2 cm) long and will begin to gain weight at a quicker pace. The eyes are now covered by full eyelids (which won't open until around 28 weeks), and the pupils and optic nerve are developing. Other facial features—nose, lips, and mouth—are also becoming more defined.

Your baby can now move her arms, legs, hands, and feet better since all of the joints work and the muscles can contract. Most of the time, though, she prefers to stay curled up.

 ## Body Update: RELAXING MOVES

Pregnant women tend to receive a lot of information and advice about exercise, but surprisingly little about the importance of relaxation. Relaxing isn't just something that helps you mentally. It has physical benefits, too.

When you relax, your body is able to rest and revive itself. Breathing slows, muscles lose their tension, stress endorphins stop racing through your system, your heart rate slows—a set of remarkable physical changes occurs known as the relaxation response. With all that your body has going on right now, giving it a chance to take a break is both restorative and healing.

Experiment to see what works for you. Some suggestions:

- Yoga. Look for a class or DVD tailored to pregnant women, if possible.

- Breathing exercises. Deep, slow breathing for just a few minutes can trigger the relaxation response.

- Meditation. If you're new to the practice or under a lot of stress, look for a course in mindfulness based stress reduction, a new popular program often taught at hospitals.

- A leisurely stroll. Relaxation doesn't have to involve any special skills.

- Massage. Avoid deep work and, ideally, find someone experienced with treating pregnant women.

- Progressive muscle relaxation. Starting at your head and, working down, tense up and then release each major muscle group.

- **Musings in solitude.** Just sit quietly and write about something positive, like your wishes for your unborn child.

Mind Update: ALL ABOARD THE EMOTIONAL ROLLER COASTER

One minute you're so excited you don't know how you can wait until your delivery day. The next, you're in tears. Emotional ups and downs are vivid during the first trimester. Blame hormones, in part. Their levels change dramatically as your baby forms and your body prepares for childbirth. Add a good bit of stress as all the pieces of your life slowly change. All this and excitement, too! It's all so dramatic—and yet so abstract, too.

What helps: recognizing that your conflicting feelings are not unusual. So what if everyone is expecting you to be glowing and cheerful 24/7 (while, for at least some of those hours, you're nauseated and conflicted)? Having some friends you can confide in can make a huge difference. Your partner may be such a person, but also sometimes he may be part of the problem on a given day. Other women who have been through pregnancy before can provide a great outlet. If you're still keeping your condition a secret, join an online community of pregnant women. (Visit a pregnancy or parenting site, such as BabyCenter.com.)

DID YOU KNOW that the father's age can be as much of a red flag for certain fetal conditions, such as Down syndrome, as the mother's? Amniocentesis is often recommended when the mother is older than 40 or the dad is older than 50.

What calms me

What brings me back to center

My entire pregnancy has been one large roller coaster ride.

AMY WEISS

Week 10

Baby Update

This week, your baby's body is about 1-1/2 inches (3.8 cm) long, with the head taking up about half of that. Weight: around 1/4 ounce (7g). Your baby's head's size and bulging shape reflect how tremendously the brain is growing and maturing. In fact, most of his vital organs have begun to function. Spinal nerves are branching out from the spinal cord.

Although you can't feel it yet, given your baby's still-minuscule size, he is very active. More big news: By the end of the week, your baby's officially known as a fetus.

Body Update: CRAVINGS

Chocolate? Peppermint ice cream? Pickled okra? It's not just folklore. Many mothers-to-be find that they hunger for particular foods early in their pregnancy. Some evolutionary biologists believe that cravings, as well as equally common aversions, are the way your pregnant body tells you which foods are desirable or not. (In caveman days, for example, meat with a strong odor might have signaled rot—not good for a baby on board.) Nobody knows for sure, but preferences are also affected by hormones and altered senses of taste and smell.

Some cravings may in fact lead you toward food choices rich in nutrients, such as fresh fruits or milk. If so, indulge! On the other hand, you may be tempted by foods that aren't so great for you or your baby. Carbs, salty foods, and spicy items are all common cravings. If so, try to limit how often or how much you indulge. Or experiment with healthier alternatives that also satisfy—such as an occasional cup of warm cocoa instead of a daily Snickers bar.

Don't beat yourself up, though, if your eating quirks aren't part of a model diet and you can't help giving in. Everybody deserves a little indulgence in pregnancy. And denying yourself completely may lead you to go overboard when you get the chance.

There's one quirky craving: that of strange substances, like chalk, clay, or laundry starch. This is called pica. It's rare, and usually caused by a dietary deficiency.

Mind Update: PICKING A NAME

You might as well start mulling the possibilities early, because sometimes it takes a full 40 weeks for a couple to agree! If you're among the lucky expectant parents who settled on a particular name for a boy and a girl long before you conceived, congratulations. Even if you're sure, though, musing on alternatives is one of the more fun pregnancy pastimes.

Among the considerations:

Do you tilt toward something original or traditional? A name that's gender specific or gender neutral? Do you want to honor someone or pick a name that reflects something meaningful to you? Will you call the child by the formal version of the name, or a nickname? Are there alternative spellings to consider? What about a middle name?

Among the places to look for ideas:

Baby name guides; online parenting sites; your family tree; historical or current public figures; favorite literary works; the Bible; TV shows, movies, or musical groups; an atlas; the telephone directory.

Then you'll have to decide whether you'll share your picks with the world before your baby is born. Some parents like to do this because they prefer to address their unborn child by his or her actual name throughout pregnancy, as a way to feel more closely bonded. (Obviously you have to wait until the gender has been confirmed.) Others prefer to wait until the name is attached to their living breathing newborn. That way friends and relatives are less likely to criticize the name.

DID YOU KNOW that once your doctor can detect your baby's heartbeat (between weeks 10 and 20, depending on method used), the risk of miscarriage drops to the low single digits (about 3 percent)?

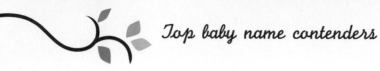

Top baby name contenders

	MY FAVORITES	MY PARTNER'S FAVORITES
Boy:	Tyler Dylan Christopher	Anthony
Girl:	Sophia Mia Olivia	

Why I like these

Likes and dislikes

New cravings

bagels

Sensitivities

pasta

I feel like some other life force has completely taken over my body. It's an amazing process, but I don't feel like that's me I'm looking at in the mirror.

LAUREN ROSEN

Week 11

Baby Update

Now 2 inches (5.1 cm) long, your baby weighs around 1/3 of an ounce (9.4 g). Under paper thin and transparent skin, the skeleton is starting to harden as bone replaces cartilage. Little toothbuds are forming under the gums (though the first tooth won't appear until 4 to 7 months old). Your baby's external genitalia are also developing. Kicks, stretches, and other movements continue to increase. He might also experience—though still imperceptible to you—bouts of hiccups, which make his entire body bounce.

Body Update: HAVE YOU KICKED CAFFEINE'S KICK?

There are some clear medical reasons some folks frown on coffee drinking in pregnancy. Caffeine interferes with the absorption of iron, draws calcium out of your body, and can possibly dehydrate you. Because it's a stimulant, caffeine can also stress your baby and prevent you from getting the rest you need. In some women, caffeine worsens heartburn, too. Though the jury's still out, some studies connect high caffeine consumption to low birth weight. At the very least, it contributes nothing nutritionally.

All that said, a cup or two of joe per day is generally considered well within safe limits. (The amount of caffeine in black tea steeped for a minute or less, or in chocolate, is not significant, unless you consume huge quantities. Check the labels of soft drinks to see how much they contain.)

Ideally, switch to decaf coffee or decaf, herbal, or green tea. Wean yourself from a serious caffeine habit with half caffeinated brews, gradually tapering off the amount of caffeinated coffee, to avoid withdrawal symptoms such as headaches and fatigue.

If you miss the energy boost you get from caffeine, try exercising more or having a protein rich snack instead. If you're used to sipping all day long, start carrying a sports bottle with water as a replacement.

Mind Update: COPING WITH WELL-INTENTIONED "ADVICE"

With all the "words of wisdom" coming your way, it's easy to feel overwhelmed, especially if you're unsure of the validity of what you hear. Before you take a truism as, well, the truth, look it up in a reputable resource or ask your doctor. He or she can also recommend references (books or Web sites) reliable for trustworthy information.

Consider three old wives' tales:

• You can tell the sex of your baby by looking for "signs."

False: Although it might be fun to guess boy or girl by examining your freckles or the position of your "bump," there's no accuracy to these methods—despite what Great Aunt Martha says.

• Stress can hurt your baby.

Semi-true: The moderate levels of stress that come with most everyday challenges—deadlines, traffic, fights with your loved ones—are unlikely to cause any harm. Most mothers-to-be don't live in placid plastic bubbles, after all. There is, however, some evidence linking extreme or prolonged stress to premature birth or low birth weight.

• You will injure your baby if you have sex.

Pretty Much False: Your baby is well protected by the amniotic sac and uterus, and therefore unaffected by intercourse. Exception: Your doctor may advise against sex in certain high-risk pregnancy situations, mostly just as a precaution.

DID YOU KNOW that certain foods can cause heartburn by relaxing the valve to your stomach? These include mint, cola, chocolate, and some teas.

Weird advice I've been given, and my advice for myself

Go ahead and ask people's advice on issues,
but then try out the answer for yourself.

ALLISON BERNAT

Week 12

The first trimester ends; the likelihood of a miscarriage drops sharply.

 ## Baby Update

Pea pod indeed! That's about how long your baby is—2-1/2 inches (6.4 cm)—with a face that's starting to organize itself into that of a newborn. The intestines, which grew so fast that they spilled into the umbilical cord, now retreat back into the abdominal cavity. Also around this time, her kidneys start excreting urine. As the nervous system continues to develop, she is demonstrating more reflexes, including sucking.

 ## Body Update: GETTING A GOOD NIGHT'S SLEEP

Even if you haven't gained much weight yet, you may find it difficult to sleep comfortably. Try these steps to get more comfortable:

- **Lie on your side.** The left side is most beneficial for your baby because it best supports the flow of blood and nutrients to the placenta.

- Curl your legs up and cross one leg over the other.

- Tuck a pillow between your legs and anywhere else that helps you feel supported and comfortable, such as under your belly or behind your back. Some mothers-to-be swear by a long body pillow.

- Around this point in your pregnancy, it's important to avoid sleeping on your back. This position exerts pressure on the inferior vena cava (a major artery), which impedes circulation, as well as on your intestines and on your back. You should also avoid stretching or exercising in this position until after you deliver.

- Fine-tune your sleep setup as your pregnancy progresses. You may want to add or rearrange support pillows as you get bigger, for example. You may also feel warmer, and therefore need fewer covers or bedclothes, or a lower thermostat setting.

Mind Update: TEST ANXIETY

Prenatal testing is a double-edged sword: Each test is an opportunity to offer reassurance that all's well, and another thing to worry about. It's certainly a normal part of pregnancy to feel anxious about your baby's well-being. And waiting for results, as well as thinking about next steps in the event of a potential problem, can be nerve-wracking.

Meet your anxiety halfway by being informed. Understand why a test is being offered to you and how and when the results will be conveyed. Be aware of the difference between a screening test (such as the triple screen), which looks for clues to the possibility of a problem, and a diagnostic test (such as amniocentesis or chorionic villus sampling), which can diagnose one.

You'll feel more confident about your baby's health by doing your part to reduce the risks and practicing basic nutrition and safety recommendations. At the same time, remind yourself that health problems are often caused by genetics or quirks of fate—not anything that the mother did or did not do. Do keep in mind that birth defects are actually very rare, and many can be corrected.

If you have intense anxiety about a particular test, talk it through with your care provider. She can help you weigh the risks and benefits through the lens of your particular situation. Be aware that it's your right to refuse a test.

DID YOU KNOW that if you've had severe nausea and been unable to gain weight, your baby is unlikely to suffer at all because the early growth can be fueled by your nutritional stores?

Ways to nurture myself

Favorite music right now

Calming music
R&B

Other favorites

*Now that I'm pregnant, I allow myself more time to do everything.
Commuting to work, I let more subway trains go by. But I'm still self-sufficient
and do a lot of things that I did before I was pregnant.*

LORI CHIARA

Musings and photos

Your Second Trimester

(13 TO 27 WEEKS)

The Middle of Everything

For most women, the middle of pregnancy is a relatively calm period. Initial adjustments and physical symptoms characteristic of the first trimester subside, while an unwieldy body and concerns about labor still lie ahead. Energy tends to pick up; nausea subsides. Your "bump," as the British say, becomes noticeable. And many women enjoy a new voluptuousness, more lush hair, and brighter skin, too. Even wearing maternity clothes can be fun. (Lose the dreary images of your mother's maternity wear; choices at every price level are so stylish and individualized now that being pregnant is not only a good excuse to get a whole new wardrobe, but also choosing it is a blast!)

Not that it's all smooth sailing. Some women continue to suffer pregnancy sickness and other complaints, or develop complications that bear watching. It's also perfectly normal to continue to feel ambivalent or apprehensive about what's happening. That's the thing about being pregnant—you have to be receptive to whatever the reality of it turns out to be for you.

You may find that your thoughts begin to shift from what's-happening-in-my-body to who's-that-in-my-body as you grow more accustomed to the physical sensations of being pregnant and begin to notice the baby move. Some mothers-to-be like to talk to their baby, refer to him or her by name (or make up a special in utero pet name), or pat their belly. Such actions are far from silly—they're the beginnings of bonding.

Becoming more aware of your baby can make it easier to make smart health choices. Talk about a powerful motivation! You are also likely to find exercise easy to manage now. Ongoing prenatal care is important to monitor your health and catch possible complications at the earliest juncture.

Second Trimester Dos and Don'ts

Do...

- Enjoy the bloom and burst of energy, as you experience them. Admire your changing shape in the mirror. Accept compliments gracefully.

- Continue taking prenatal vitamins.

- Be sure to consume enough protein. Your body needs it to help fuel your baby's development. Think broadly about possible sources, including such meatless choices as tofu and other soy products, wheat germ, nuts, cheese, and the countless variety of beans available.

- Use common sense when exercising. Stretch beforehand. Quit when you become over-exerted and don't allow yourself to become overheated. Drink water before and after your workout. If you're too sick or tired to exercise, don't force it; give yourself an occasional break.

- Take advantage of the "sexy surge" if it happens to you. Surging hormones often make women feel especially frisky in the middle months. Consider it one of the fringe benefits of pregnancy.

- Travel, if you can. Chances are that you feel good and, if you get a positive bill of health, can enjoy time alone or with your partner in a fairly unencumbered way.

- Wear a seat belt in the car every time. Position the lap strap just below your belly and the diagonal strap between your breasts. Make sure they both fit snugly.

- Enjoy your partner. Go to a movie, throw a (low-key) party, dine out, plan a second honeymoon (sometimes called a "babymoon").

Don't...

- **Eat for two.** Nope, still not true.

- **Believe everything you hear.** There's nothing like a visibly pregnant woman to invite advice, comments, and strange-but-supposedly true tales of how to determine an unborn baby's gender, health, or personality. Take everything you're told by well-intentioned (but not necessarily medically trained) observers with two grains of salt.

- **Expect to feel like anybody else.** Comparing notes with other pregnant women can be helpful, but only to a point. The range of symptoms and issues is so broad and individualized that it's impossible to tell you how you should be feeling at any given time.

- **Leave your primary ob-gyn doctor out of the loop.** If you become interested in an alternative therapy, whether it's a botanical product, hypnosis, acupuncture, sound therapy, or something else, consult your doctor or midwife. These treatments can work with, or against, your conventional medical treatment. Ideally, those treating you should be on the same page. Be aware that some alternative therapies are unstudied in pregnancy.

- **Overdo it.** Now's a season for lightening your overall load, not adding to it. Take breaks more often than you used to, and make sure you get at least 7 to 8 hours sleep at night.

- **Skip obstetric visits if you feel fine.** It's important for your health and your baby's to be monitored at the regular intervals recommended by your doctor or midwife.

What I'm thinking about

Questions for my health professional

*In months one through five, I felt excited, but also sad and a little depressed.
I could see changes beginning to happen to my body and gained a little weight.
But my pregnancy still was not evident to the outside world so my enthusiasm
could not be shared with others. At times I just felt fat.*

MARY ANN KENDALL

Week 13

Good news! Expect nausea to suddenly lift as hCG levels stabilize.

 ## Baby Update

Measuring about 3 inches (7.6 cm) and weighing around 1 ounce (23.4 g), your baby looks a bit like a miniature—a very miniature—newborn. The little body is fully formed, though his head is still disproportionately large. His kidneys and urinary tract are fully functioning this week: He can swallow and expel amniotic fluid. Most of the critical development of the organs and body systems is complete; the likelihood of a miscarriage decreases significantly from this point on. One tiny detail is also complete—your baby even has unique fingerprints.

 ## Body Update: DENTAL CARE

Some women believe they should avoid the dentist during pregnancy. To the contrary, keeping your mouth clean and healthy is important for both you and your baby. A surprising number of infections begin orally. Some women do prefer to schedule a checkup during the second trimester, though, once morning sickness abates and the greatest threat of miscarriage has passed.

There are some precautions you should take. Avoid X-rays if possible, but if you need to have them done, wear a lead shield for protection. Also, if you need dental work beyond a regular cleaning, discuss the safety of the procedure and the anesthesia it requires with your obstetrician beforehand; some procedures can be easily postponed until after delivery.

Regular dental care at home is important, too. Brush your teeth (and gums) with a soft-bristle brush and floss regularly. Gums tend to be more sensitive and bleed more easily in pregnancy, but don't let that stop you from regular care.

Mind Update: SELF-NECESSITIES

Given all the focus on your baby, what have you done for *yourself* lately? Often, when pregnant women do something nice for themselves, it's in the name of the baby: eating right, making time for exercise, and so on. That's all well and good. But you might as well use these waning pre-motherhood months to lavish attention on yourself, too.

Every day, resolve to do one little thing that's just for you, just for fun, just because. Some ideas:

- Arrange fresh flowers in a vase (from your garden or from the grocery).

- Serve your juice in a fancy wineglass.

- Buy new silly socks.

- Spend 10 minutes reading a trashy novel or entertaining magazine before bed.

- Get a massage, or ask someone to give you one.

- Eat one square of your favorite chocolate on Sunday afternoons.

- Try a new flavor of tea.

- Drive to a neighborhood you've never been in before, park, and walk.

- Buy a new lipstick.

- Slip into a matinee and eat popcorn.

- Apply a perfume that you usually save for special occasions.

- Experiment with a bright scarf or pretty earrings to jazz up a basic maternity top.

- Burn a special CD of favorite songs for your pregnancy, or ask your partner to load some new surprises onto your iPod.

- Paint your nails.

- Shave your legs, and not just the visible parts.

- Soak in the tub with scented oils, candles—the whole elaborate deal.

- Turn off your cell for a designated amount of "quiet time."

- Nap. Nap. Nap!

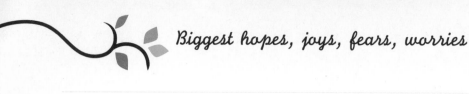

Biggest hopes, joys, fears, worries

If pregnancy were a book they would cut the last two chapters.

NORA EPHRON

Week 14

 ## Baby Update

Your baby's head is looking more and more proportional, mostly because the rest of the body is growing more rapidly now. This week, she is about 3-1/2 inches (8.9 cm) long, and weighs around 1-1/2 ounces (42.5 g). A fuzzy layer of fine hair, called lanugo, is beginning to coat her entire body. Internally, the liver is starting to secrete bile, and the spleen is helping produce red blood cells. And, as the brain continues to mature, she can make different facial expressions and may even react when someone gives your belly a little poke.

 ## Body Update: BREAKING OUT?

Many mothers-to-be experience bouts of acne, the likes of which they haven't seen since their teenage years. The same culprits are at fault now as were then—raging hormones, specifically estrogen and progesterone. Hormones may also cause heavier perspiration, causing heat rashes.

For acne-prone skin, use a gentle cleanser and remove any makeup completely before going to bed. Try switching to cosmetics and personal care products made for sensitive skin. Consult with your doctor about over-the-counter medications, but avoid Accutane and Retin-A, which have been linked to birth defects. Cornstarch is helpful to keep heat rash-prone skin cool and dry.

You may also notice small, very fine red lines that seem to branch out under your skin on your face and neck. These are vascular spiders (spider nevi) and are completely harmless. There isn't much you can do about them, but they will disappear after childbirth.

Mind Update: FEELING SCATTERBRAINED?

Losing your keys. Forgetting a colleague's name. Walking upstairs to get . . . something, what was it again? Many pregnant women experience a sensation of memory loss and distraction. There is a lot on your mind, after all. Sleep disruptions, stress, and possibly hormonal changes can contribute to spacey feelings.

Forgetfulness can be disruptive and frustrating.

Try these memory crutches:

- Take notes in a special notebook (or this journal). Jot down everything from to-do lists to payment due dates to information that you would normally know off the top of your head (such as frequently used phone numbers). Keeping all this information in one location is handy.

- Use technology to your advantage. Make your life easier by signing up for electronic bill pay options that automatically withdraw funds from your bank account, for example. Store new pregnancy-related phone numbers in your cell, including your care provider and your favorite maternity store.

- Write down appointments and meetings in a full-size calendar (and in the date book you carry), and hang it somewhere prominent. It's especially important to keep your doctor's appointments.

- Don't hide it—confide it. Talk about the difficulty you're having with someone close to you. You may find that she has suggestions that could help you stay organized, or at least she could give you some reassurance and support.

- Give yourself a break. Minimize multitasking and don't take on too much at one time. Simplify as best you can, and make sure you take some time to rest and relax.

DID YOU KNOW that you lose fewer hairs in pregnancy, making your mane seem thicker?

How I feel about my appearance and weight

How I feel about carrying my baby

I loved being pregnant! I thought it was beautiful, and though I hated to see the scale going up in numbers, I felt that what I had growing inside of me offset the weight gain in every way.

AMY WEISS

Week 15

Baby Update

Your baby is about 4 inches (10.2 cm) long and weighs around 2 ounces (56.7 g). The limbs are getting longer now, especially the legs. His bones are starting to store calcium, or to ossify, which means that you could see his skeleton with an X-ray.

At the same time, your baby's ears are looking more "human" and the eyes are moving closer together. (They started out far on the sides of his head.) Vision is developing even though the eyes remain closed. He can tell the difference between darkness and bright light around your belly, though.

Body Update: BEATING DIETARY DOLDRUMS

Getting tired of eating the same old nutritious things day after day? Spice up your diet with the occasional meal or snack that's unconventional for you. Dig through cookbooks or cooking magazines for ideas, even if you're not normally the foodie type. Ask your friends what they prepare when they want something "different."

A few ideas:

- Breakfast mixes. Fill a tortilla with scrambled eggs, cheese, ham, and vegetables or load an omelet with vegetables. Scoop fruit and yogurt onto pancakes, waffles, or cereal.

- Breakfast breads for snacks. Banana or zucchini bread is a hearty way to add vegetables. Eat it plain or with a spread of nut butter.

- Multiflavored pizza. Pizza can be a good choice because it provides grain, dairy, and vegetables. Experiment with different toppings: salsa; grated bell peppers, carrots, or zucchini; spinach; a little cheddar; bean sprouts; tofu—almost anything goes.

- Drink up nutrients. Keep hydrated with wholesome fruit smoothies made with milk, yogurt, or soy milk.

- Make the most of dessert. Try a delicious parfait with layers of yogurt, granola, and fresh fruit. Sample different flavors of frozen fruit bars or sorbet.

Mind Update: COMPARING NOTES

"You already felt your baby move?" "You mean you never felt sick or fat, ever?" As your pregnancy progresses, you may find yourself comparing yourself with other women. Comparing notes can be good: you can share how you're feeling; ask one another questions; and share advice, support, and encouragement. But there's a potential downside, if judging yourself against someone else causes you to worry needlessly or feel like there's something "wrong" with you.

Remember that each pregnancy is different. The discomforts you feel, your weight gain, and your attitude toward medical care, nutrition, and other issues can be very different from someone else's (even your own mother's or your best friend's). Keep an open mind, but trust your instincts and talk to your doctor if you have any concerns.

Self-care measures

*Because the discomforts of pregnancy sometimes overshadowed
the happy anticipation, I made it a point to self-nurture with
little treats, quiet time, and cat naps.*

JOYCE WALKER

Week 16

 ## Baby Update

The amount of fine-tuning that's taken place in the last month is nothing short of miraculous. Your baby now measures about 4-1/2 inches (11.4 cm) and weighs around 3 ounces (85.1 g). She's just beginning a growth spurt.

She moves a lot, from stretches to kicks to turns, which get successively stronger as she gets stronger and bigger.

 ## Body Update: WAS THAT IT?!

Few things make you stop and take notice like the first time you think you feel your baby move inside you. Most women first become aware of this sensation, called "quickening," when they're about 16 to 22 weeks along. If you're slender, it can happen as early as 15 weeks.

The movement hits you just below the navel. It may feel like a soft nudge, a gas bubble or bubbles, or like being brushed from the inside by a flutter of wings. It's generally not for a few more weeks, when the baby grows and gets stronger, that you notice more decisive kicks and bumps. These "kicks" as they're collectively known, are intermittent, rather than constant. But sometimes so many movements will happen in quick succession that it'll seem like your little one is working out.

For many women, pregnancy becomes far more "real" once they've felt movement. How does it feel to you? Do you feel different about your baby now? Bear in mind, though, that your partner may not be able to feel movements for a few more weeks—while you're experiencing them from the inside, he can feel them only from the outside.

Mind Update: TOP MID-PREGNANCY WORRIES

Every mother-to-be worries about something. Having a baby is such a huge unknown, it's only natural to play "what if" and "omigosh!"

Here are a few frets that tend to cause more anxiety than they warrant:

- **Fear of miscarriage.** The weeks between when morning sickness ends but you haven't yet felt the baby move can be spooky: how do you know you're still pregnant? In the absence of bleeding or pain, everything's probably just fine. Confide your worries to your doctor at your next visit, if you can't shake the feeling.

- **Fear of falls.** It's possible, because your center of gravity is changing. But even if you do tumble, you're unlikely to harm your baby. Go slowly and carefully, and avoid foolish moves like standing on stepladders to stash boxes in upper cupboards.

- **Fear of health problems in your baby.** Birth defects are rare in the overall population, but testing can help ease worries. If you have specific reason for concern, such as family history, talk to your doctor about additional genetic testing.

- **Fear of being a lousy mother.** The mere fact that you're thinking about this subject indicates that you want to do right by your baby and be a good parent. Whether you want to raise your child differently from how you were brought up, or just the same, looking at different role models and considering how you'll be are all cause for pats on the back, not anxiety attacks.

DID YOU KNOW that pregnant skin tends toward dryness? Be faithful about moisturizing and using sunscreen, too.

Nursery plans & ideas

Life is tough enough without having someone kick you from the inside.

RITA RUDNER

Musings and photos

Week 17

Baby Update

This week your baby is about 4-3/4 inches (12.1 cm) long and weighs about 4-1/2 ounces (127.6 g). Now that the body parts are in place, his body is starting to "fill out" as he develops fat tissue. Bones continue to harden slowly, and joints are becoming more functional.

Now that the ears are positioned appropriately on the sides of the head, his hearing develops. Also starting now, your baby's umbilical cord is getting thicker and stronger (eventually it will be so tough, it'll take real effort to cut the cord after birth).

Body Update: COMFORT FOR LEG CRAMPS

Starting in your second trimester, you may feel sharp cramps in your legs. Some people call the pain in your thigh or calf a "charley horse." It's often felt when you're lying in bed or have been standing for a long time. These cramps may be the result of increasing pressure on your legs' nerves or a lack of calcium or magnesium.

To prevent cramps and find relief when they occur:

- Stretch your calf muscles by gently lunging (one foot forward) to a wall, keeping your feet flat on the floor and your back and the leg that's behind you straight (don't bounce).

- Avoid standing or sitting in one place for too long. If you have to stand awhile, try wearing support hose.

- Add foods rich in calcium, magnesium, and/or potassium to your diet.

- Extend your leg and stretch your foot (with toes pointed up) when you get a cramp.

- More Rx: Softly massage your leg or apply a heating pad to the affected area.

Mind Update: BOY OR GIRL?

Because of improved ultrasound and the increased use of sonograms and other prenatal tests, it's almost more work *not* to find out your baby-to-be's gender. The vast majority of parents want to know, according to polls. Just because you *can* find out doesn't mean that you *have* to know, however.

Here are some pros to finding out:

- You can narrow down your choices for a name.
- You may feel like it's easier to bond with your baby.
- You can buy or ask for gender-specific nursery decorations, clothing, and toys.

Here are some cons to finding out:

- You can daydream about the possibilities (which may help distract you from some of your stress and anxiety).
- You can buy and receive neutral clothing and gifts that may be handed down to other babies, regardless of their sex.
- You will have one more thing to be excited about when your baby is born.

If you do decide not to find out, be sure to remind your doctor at every visit so she doesn't slip, and emphatically inform nurses and technicians at screenings and other times they are looking at your records in your presence. Most professionals will cheerfully abide by your wishes, but the extra reminders really help.

How I feel about having a boy or a girl

A small seed with a spirit was forming inside of me.
It was now my job to nurture this living thing.

DIANE LEWIS

Week 18

 ## Baby Update

Your baby has grown to about 5-1/2 inches (13.4 cm) and weighs around 5-1/2 ounces (156 g). If your baby is a boy, his genitals have grown such that they may be visible with an ultrasound; if your baby is a girl, her fully formed fallopian tubes and uterus are now where they should be. Another interesting thing that can be seen on ultrasound: thumb sucking!

 ## Body Update: SEX AND THE NURSERY

Chances are your sexual desire is changing—for reasons that could include hormones, a more positive or negative body image, your partner's attitudes, fatigue, discomfort, and other conditions. You may want sex more, surprising yourself at how much you day-dream or fantasize about it. This may be especially true if it's become easier for you to experience an orgasm (due to hormones and increased blood flow). Alternatively, you may want it less, dreading even the suggestion of foreplay. Many pregnant women say their desire peaks during the second trimester.

If you are interested (and as long as your doctor doesn't warn you against it), sexual intimacy is a great, safe way to nurture your relationship with your partner. Communicate sincerely with him—it's likely you both have concerns and preferences to consider. You may feel more comfortable in certain positions than in others, for example on top or on your side. And when you find your interest is down, be honest. Even if your desire has gone up in general, it may dip some days.

If you have any concerns, such as pain or bleeding caused by intercourse, be sure to talk to your doctor.

Mind Update: PREGNANT DREAMS

Have you been surprised by a particularly vivid, strange dream or frightening nightmare lately? Some pregnant women dream of their baby in bewildering forms (a piglet? A loaf of bread?). A common dream has a woman forgetting to care for her child. These kinds of sleep images can occur frequently during pregnancy—and no, they're not omens that you're going to be a terrible mother! Your mind is trying to cope with a lot of information as you undergo significant physical and emotional changes and as you anticipate the lifestyle changes coming your way. It's logical that your mind would work overtime then, sorting things out as you sleep.

One bright side: At this point in pregnancy, you are more likely to wake up during REM sleep (light, or dream sleep) now. That makes it more likely you can remember your dreams. They can be fun to puzzle over. For example, a dream about losing the baby may help you deal with a fear of miscarriage that you would rather ignore when you're awake. You may dream about your competence (or imagined lack thereof) in taking care of a "bun in the oven." Your protective maternal instinct may also creep up in dreams in which you and your baby are threatened (as during a crime or accident).

If you can't figure out what's behind your dreams and they're causing you considerable stress, try doing a little research in a book about dreams and their meanings. Sometimes a therapist, if you are seeing one, can help you tease out interpretations.

Dreams

I dreamed I had triplets and that I forgot the babies at home when I went to work.
The shift from being a working woman to being a working mother—
and the awesome responsibility that would entail—tugged at my psyche.

JOYCE WALKER

Week 19

Most mothers-to-be have felt the baby move by now; if you haven't, give it a few more weeks.

Baby Update

Although your baby still weighs less than a pound, she's getting heavier as fat stores increase. Your baby measures about 6 inches (15.2 cm) this week. Hair appears, on the head and as eyebrows and eyelashes. And even though they won't make their debut until years from now, her permanent teeth buds are developing under the gums, behind the milk teeth (baby teeth) buds. Also this week, your baby's brain is assigning specific areas to support each of the five senses.

Brace yourself for ever more gymnastics. Beyond kicks and stretches, your baby may flip upside down, twist and roll from side to side. Later in pregnancy, though, these movements won't be so dramatic because there will be less space in the uterus for them.

Body Update: SLEEPUS INTERRUPTUS?

Getting a good night's rest can become challenging. Many women find they have to rise often to use the bathroom. Fetal movements, an inability to get comfortable, and a racing mind can all add to sleep trouble.

Ten tips:

- **Keep it routine.** Try to go to bed and get up at about the same time every day and night.

- **Make your room sleep friendly.** Lose the TV set, turn off the radio, keep the room dark and free of distractions.

- Check your caffeine intake and cut back.

- Eliminate or shorten naps by day if you're having trouble sleeping at night.

- Try keeping the room on the cool side.

- **Get plenty of exercise and fresh air by day.** Even sitting outdoors can help.

- Consume as few liquids as possible after dinner, so you're less likely to have to get up and disrupt your sleep.

- If waking to urinate isn't a problem, try a cup of warm milk or green tea with cinnamon or chamomile flavoring, to help induce sleep.

- When you find yourself ruminating on something, stop and think about something happy, like your baby's first birthday party. Corny, but it works.

- Change bed linens often. Fresh crisp percale or soft flannels can make your bed more inviting—and don't forget the supportive pillows!

 ## Mind Update: INVOLVING YOUR PARTNER

It's natural that you become the center of attention as family and friends—and even strangers—rally around the "visible" baby you're carrying.

Help your partner avoid feeling left out:

- Bring him along to your doctor's appointments.

- Encourage him to start forming a bond with your baby by feeling your belly for kicks and talking or reading to your baby.

- Talk together about your hopes for your baby, guess what your baby might be like, and reminisce about your own childhoods.

- Shop for baby gear and furniture together. Let him assemble the crib!

- Involve him in all major decisions—from baby names to medical care.

- Invite him to exercise with you.

- Attend childbirth, breast-feeding, and other classes together.

- Listen to each other's fears and concerns.

How I nurture my relationship with my partner

My husband was happy and ready to take on the new experience,
so that made it easier for me to deal with my apprehensions.
A supportive spouse helps more than you can imagine.

CASSANDRA BELL

Week 20

Congratulations! You're halfway to motherhood!

Baby Update: THE MIDWAY POINT!

Now that your baby has stretched his legs out a bit, his length is measured from the crown of his head to his heel. The average fetus is now about 9-1/2 inches (24.1 cm) long and weighs around 9 ounces (255 g). A smooth white layer of *vernix caseosa*, a natural substance that's like baby's first moisturizer, covers your baby's body to protect the skin while living submerged in its watery home.

Also around this time, he starts converting waste into dark and sticky meconium, a "pre-poop" that will probably test your skills as a baby wiper during your first few diaper changes.

Body Update: BACK CARE

One side effect of your growing baby and expanding uterus is a shifting center of gravity. Your back works extra hard to provide support—no wonder it aches sometimes!

You can protect your spine and back muscles by being especially careful to use good posture, and follow these tips.

* When you walk: Keep your shoulders back and your spine as straight as possible. Most women find the most comfort wearing low, supportive heels (1/2 inch to 2 inches, or 1 to 5 cm), rather than high heels or complete flats.

* When you sit: Sit with your back straight and legs uncrossed. If you have to stand or sit in one place for long periods, such as at work, elevate one of your feet on a low stool. At a desk, sit directly facing your paperwork or computer. Try using a pillow to support the small of your back.

* When you sleep: Don't lie flat on your back. Make sure you have a firm mattress; if yours is more than 10 years old, this is a good opportunity to upgrade.

* When you lift: Stand with your feet apart, bend at your knees (not your waist), and let your arms and legs do the work.

- Relieve your backache with these feel-good exercises:

- Stand with your back and shoulders against a wall. Tighten your abdominal muscles and gently pull your stomach in and tilt the pelvis upward. Hold that position for about 5 seconds. Return to the starting position. This "pelvic tilt" can also be done lying on the floor with your legs partly bent, feet flat on the floor.

- Get on all fours, with your hands flat on the floor and your back straight. Tighten your abdominal muscles and gently curl your lower back upward, like a cat. Hold that position for about 5 seconds. Return to the starting position.

- Put your hands on your shoulders and roll your elbows front to back.

 ## Mind Update: FEELING LESS THAN PERFECT

So you weigh more than you expected you would by this point in pregnancy. Or you already have stretch marks. You're sick of everyone yammering about the baby and how excited you must be—and you feel guilty for feeling this way. You don't know how you can possibly make it all the way until your due date. Point is, everybody can find something about their pregnancy that's off-key, not quite what they expected.

What to do about it?

- Repeat over and over: There is no such thing as a perfect pregnancy.

- Go with the flow. Some days are smooth, others feel like you're shooting the rapids. Consider it preparation for motherhood.

- Don't ask, "Why me?" Some women get stretch marks now, some get colicky babies later. The universe isn't fair, and neither is pregnancy. So pamper yourself!

DID YOU KNOW that, for some women, significant fatigue continues well into the second trimester?

What makes me happy

I felt like a part of a huge happy community of women.
Even in New York City, strangers talked to me as if I were their cousin.

RISA MAY

Musings and photos

Week 21

 Baby Update: HELLO, BIG BOY OR GIRL!

Your baby is now about 10 inches (25.4 cm) long and weighs around 10-1/2 ounces (297.7 g). The digestive system is maturing; while swallowing amniotic fluid your baby absorbs some water and nutrients from it. If your baby is a girl, her fully formed vagina is also continuing to develop.

Your baby is getting plenty of exercise inside of you and you might wonder if your baby is a night owl based on its "schedule." The truth is all of your movement throughout the day likely rocks your baby to sleep, so when you go to bed, your baby's raring to go.

 Body Update: WEIGHT GAIN

It's natural to wonder if your weight gain is going well. The "typical" pregnancy results in a weight gain of 25 to 35 pounds (about 2 to 2-1/2 stones). But our culture is so conditioned to think negatively about weight gain in general, it can be hard for a woman to keep perspective. Baby weight, within reason, is good weight! Your baby cannot thrive without it!

After the initial 3 or 4 pounds (1.4 or 1.8 kg) gained in the first trimester, most women add about a pound (454 g) a week during the last two trimesters. That's only a very rough rule of thumb—not a prescription! Your doctor can help you monitor your weight and make sure it's healthy for you and your baby.

Here's a breakdown of how the weight of a typical 30-pound (13.6-kg) gain is distributed:

Baby = 7-1/2 pounds (3.4 kg)   Placenta = 1-1/2 pounds (680 g)
Amniotic fluid = 2 pounds (907 g) Uterus = 2 pounds (907 g)
Breasts = 2 pounds (907 g)   Body stores = 7 pounds (3.18 kg)
Blood = 4 pounds (1.8 kg)   Other body fluids = 4 pounds (1.8 kg)

Your doctor may encourage you to gain less if you were overweight pre-pregnancy, or more if you were underweight.

Mind Update: WHAT TO WEAR

Never before have women had such a variety of options for comfortable and fashionable maternity clothes.

When building your new wardrobe:

- **Choose some basic pieces that you can mix and match.** Look for black, navy, or khaki slacks, skirt, and cardigan. Most women like comfy maternity jeans.

- **Give yourself some room to grow.** Pick clothes that fit well now, but have some room. Believe it or not it is possible to outgrow a roomy maternity top before you deliver. Stretch fabrics and adjustable features, like a tie in back of a blouse, help.

- **Find a dress or outfit that you can dress up with accessories for special events.** Few things are more frustrating than trying to find something extra nice to wear—that still fits—in your closet at the last minute.

- **Browse your partner's wardrobe.** A man's plain white button-down shirt is a very versatile shirt or jacket, for example.

- **Borrow from friends and family, or check consignment shops.** A new mother can be a pregnant woman's best friend.

- **Update your underwear drawer too, as needed.** Good fit and support in a bra are very important, and you might feel better in roomier undies.

- **Help keep your body temperature comfortable by choosing natural fibers, like cotton or silk, and lightweight fabrics that you can layer.**

- **Avoid overbuying.** You will only need maternity clothes for a limited time. If budget is an issue, select good quality pieces that you can use often. Some shirts and bras designed for nursing mothers can do double duty now and later.

DID YOU KNOW that there is no standard "look" for a pregnant belly? Some women carry higher or lower than others, stick out more in front, or barely seem to show at all by mid-pregnancy.

What makes me feel emotional

What concerns me

Sometimes I miss my old self.

LANA HEADLEY

Week 22

 ## Baby Update

This week your baby is about 10-1/2 inches (26.7 cm) long and weighs around 13 ounces (368.5 g). Despite the padding your baby is acquiring, filling out occurs slowly, so it still looks a little wrinkly. The skin is so thin that you can see a network of blood vessels underneath it. But her facial features are more visible now, including minuscule lips, fully formed eyelids, and fine eyebrows. Some parents are surprised at how distinctive the features may appear on an ultrasound. Her eyes are also fully formed, though pigment has yet to color them. Also around this time, your baby's liver and pancreas continue to develop.

 ## Body Update: KICK COUNTS

Your baby's athletics are more than entertaining. They provide reassurance that all's well. (A baby who has stopped moving for long periods may be asleep, or, much less likely, may have become tangled in the umbilical cord or have another problem.) For this reason, doctors recommend that expectant mothers monitor their baby's movements periodically through the day. You don't have to be obsessive about this. It's simply a matter of pausing to pay attention.

Your doctor or midwife may suggest her preferred method. A simple way: Choose a starting time and begin counting movements. Once you reach 10, note the time and calculate the number of minutes it took. If you don't reach 10 in an hour, have a snack or a glass of juice and try again.

If you have any concerns about your baby's activity or you notice fewer than 10 movements in an hour (after eating a snack or drinking juice), notify your doctor. There are simple noninvasive tests that can be done in the office to stimulate movement and further assess fetal well-being.

Mind Update: HANDLING UNWANTED ADVICE

A swelling belly is like a magnet for advice givers, drawing them to you with ever so helpful tips, suggestions, and admonishments. Or not so helpful, as the case may be. "Your heels are too high!" "That coffee is bad for your baby!" "I saw a great gizmo you need for your baby!" "Did you know that . . ."

How to cope?

- **First, consider the source.** Women who have had children before you are founts of knowledge. So don't dismiss all advice automatically. Sometimes the tips of someone experienced can save you time or money, for example. Remember most people are just trying to help.

- **Forgive them their trespasses.** In their excitement over your condition, friends and strangers alike tend to overstep boundaries without realizing it, saying things to a pregnant woman (like, "Don't you know doughnuts have little nutritional value?") that they'd never dream of saying to someone who wasn't pregnant. Chalk it up to good intentions. It's their way of showing that they care.

- **Politely ignore the dubious and the dangerous.** Told about an herb potion sure to vanquish stretch marks or an exercise regimen you aren't sure about? Say something benign like, "That sounds interesting; I'll ask my doctor." If your persistent counselor asks later why you haven't been doing what they suggested, blame your ob: "My doctor would rather I not try that."

- **Cut out when you've had enough.** When the advice expands from a comment to a torrent, or turns into nagging, sometimes you just need to offer a cool, "Thanks for your interest," and change the subject. Ask a mother her opinions about something benign like nursery decorations. Or excuse yourself to use the restroom (yet again!).

DID YOU KNOW that numerous studies have proven ultrasound to be safe?

What feels new this week

Being pregnant is a humbling experience, as you realize how much smarter your body is than your mind.

BARBARA PAULDING

Week 23

 ## Baby Update

About 11 inches (27.9 cm) long, your baby now weighs a grand total of approximately 1 pound (453.6 g). As he gains weight and moves around, muscles are being strengthened. Air sacs (alveoli) and blood vessels are also developing in the lungs just about now, getting your baby ready to breathe. However, the lungs would still be too immature to do the job on their own and if he was born now, mechanical support would be required. Even though he won't actually breathe air until birth, he "practices" by inhaling and exhaling amniotic fluid.

The hearing is also improving. Your baby may begin to grow accustomed to the usual loud noises produced by your body or around your home. Some people believe that listening to music calms a fetus. Certainly, by birth, your fetus will have come to recognize your distinctive voice. (It's even been said that babies in the womb who hear a dog bark will be less likely to be spooked as newborns.)

 ## Body Update: QUICK NUTRITIOUS SNACK IDEAS

Find yourself ransacking the cupboards looking for something to eat? Many women find that they prefer small mini-meals as their digestive system begins to be rearranged by the expanding uterus.

Good-for-you snacks help satisfy nibbles without guilt:

- Add natural or chunky peanut butter to other foods, such as apple slices, mini carrots, bagel chips, or celery sticks.

- Mix fresh or canned fruit (in its own juice, not syrup) with cottage cheese.

- Stock up on healthy finger foods that you can eat on the go, such as seedless grapes.

- Sample different cereals, or mix several kinds together. Best: fortified, low-sugar options that you can eat as finger food.

- Treat yourself to exotic fruits you don't usually buy, like mangoes, papayas, and kiwi. Try them with some vanilla yogurt.

- **Make a roll-up.** Spread cream cheese (and mashed avocado if you like) on a thin tortilla or flat bread. Pile on thin slices of vegetables, such as cucumber, tomato, and onion, and roll it up. Chop the roll into bite-size segments.

Mind Update: REACH OUT AND (DON'T) TOUCH ME!

You may begin to notice an interesting phenomenon: The more you show, the more inclined people are to want to rub your belly! It is hard to ignore, after all. Some women aren't bothered by this, and even welcome the chance to share their pregnancy in this way. Others grow irritated or take offense at having their personal boundary crossed.

The touchers, though, rarely see themselves as being rude or intrusive. They imagine themselves touching not you but the baby. Your belly is a happy, outward sign of fertility and you are, well, a sort of lucky Buddha. Even the most tolerant mothers-to-be might understandably draw the line at having their maternity top raised by an eager patter.

If you've had enough, it's your pregnant prerogative to say, "I'd rather you didn't do that," or "Please stop; it's not comfortable." The belly-patter won't know if you're referring to your feelings or your physical state, and if upsetting you doesn't motivate him to cease and desist, the idea of doing anything that might be bad for the baby usually does the trick.

Some mothers try to deflect the situation with humor: "Look, but don't touch." Or, "You can pat mine if I can pat yours."

The many moods of me

Pregnancy was the most mentally and physically challenging event of my life.

JENNIFER GARRETT

Week 24

Most women have a glucose screening between 24 and 28 weeks to screen for the need for further testing for gestational diabetes.

Baby Update

This week your baby is almost at the 1-foot (30.5 cm) mark. Average weight: about 1-1/4 pounds (567 g). It's a time of "more of the same." The brain continues to develop. (That organ in particular will be only partially "online" at birth, and requires the first 3 years of life to wire up, in terms of how sight, sound, and other stimuli are fully processed.) The lungs are branching out and developing cells to make *surfactant*, which helps the air sacs inflate. His taste buds are also under development now.

Your baby still moves quite a bit, even though the amniotic sac is becoming somewhat of a tight fit. The amniotic fluid allows him to move safely and relatively easily.

Body Update: BELLY BASICS

As the skin on your abdomen stretches, you may begin to feel some itchiness. This is normal. Try not to scratch or you could make the dry skin feel even worse. Instead, try using some moisturizer or shea butter (applying it as soon as you step out of the shower). Avoid soap that dries your skin.

At the same time, you may start to notice thin pink, reddish or purplish lines branching out across your abdomen. Although some creams and lotions promise to prevent or reduce the appearance of stretch marks, none have been proven to work. You may be able to prevent them somewhat by gaining weight gradually and within your recommended range. These marks will likely fade significantly or disappear completely on their own with time. If they last longer than six months postpartum and they bother you very much, talk to a dermatologist.

Mind Update: OLD WIVES' TALES

"Young wives" tell them, too. Old wives' tales are superstitious beliefs rooted in folklore, and pregnancy is rife with them. They can be fun to think about, if you don't take them too seriously. Or you can just safely ignore them—no matter how persistently a little old lady in the supermarket may try to insist upon their veracity.

Here are some golden oldies that are NOT true:

If you have a lot of heartburn, your baby will have a lot of hair. Acne signals a girl because she's thought to be stealing your beauty. Eating strawberries causes reddish birthmarks. Cutting your hair during pregnancy robs a fetus of its energy. If you go swimming you might drown the baby. Craving sweets means a boy; craving sours means a girl. Worrying too much in pregnancy will give you a boy. Boys are more active in the womb. Don't lift your arms above your head or you might cause a knot in the umbilical cord. Young children can predict your baby's gender. Carrying high means it's a girl; carrying low indicates a boy.

Interestingly, there are a few "clichés of pregnancy" that ARE true:

Pregnancy makes your feet grow. Thank the hormone relaxin, which loosens all your joints in order to prepare your pelvis for delivery.

Labor often starts at night. The production of oxytocin, a hormone that causes contractions, peaks in the evening.

Second babies are easier to deliver. Second labors tend to be shorter on average than first labors because the muscles involved have already stretched some and your pelvic bones may be wider. If your firstborn was delivered by C-section, however, your next labor is more likely to progress like a first-timer's.

DID YOU KNOW that babies nap in utero?

Plans and hopes for the baby

Your top job as a new parent is to love your baby like crazy.

HARVEY KARP, MD

Musings and photos

Week 25

Baby Update

Your baby is about 12-1/2 inches (31.8 cm) long and weighs around 1-1/2 pounds (680.4 g). She is slowly on the way to looking more like a cuddly newborn as her body bulks up with more baby fat. But more important, growing a good layer of fat tissue will help her regulate her own body temperature outside the womb and will provide energy. This week your baby might also show off a particular hair color and texture (but these could change after birth and she might lose this first head of hair altogether).

Body Update: READYING FOR CHILDBIRTH

A simple, almost effortless way to prepare your body to support and, later, deliver your baby is to strengthen your pelvic floor muscles.

There are several methods:

- **Kegels:** These exercises are very easy and nobody can tell you're doing it: Just tighten up as if you were stopping a flow of urine, and hold for 5 seconds. (But don't actually practice while you're urinating as this can cause an infection.) Start with 5 Kegels, 5 times a day and work up to 10 Kegels, 10 times a day. You can also later increase the number of seconds you hold to 10. An even more advanced technique is to contract your muscles in "steps" and then slowly relax one step at a time (this is sometimes called the elevator Kegel).

- **Tailor sitting:** This exercise prepares your groin and upper legs. Get into position as if you were going to sit cross-legged on the floor. Instead of crossing your ankles, though, pull one ankle into your body and pull the other one just in front of it. Alternately, you can bring the soles of your feet together. Then lean forward slightly so your knees almost reach the floor. Hold this for as long as you can without straining (try for 2 minutes at a time, several times a day).

- **Squats.** These help widen your pelvic opening and also work your legs. With your hands on a piece of furniture for support, stand with your feet apart (a little wider than your hips) and your toes pointed slightly outward. Bend your legs, keeping your back straight and your heels on the floor, and lower into a sitting position. Exhale as you stretch your legs to return to standing position.

Mind Update: STORIES YOU'D RATHER NOT HEAR

Everybody, it seems, has a birth story to share—not always their own, but some long saga that happened to their cousin, sister, or someone else. Hearing such stories can help you prepare for your own experience. But "horror" stories can cause you needless anxiety. Don't underestimate how a story might affect you. It may "roll off your back" now, but may spook you when you're feeling stressed out.

Here are some tips for dealing with unwanted stories:

- Before the person gets too far, smile and candidly ask, "This isn't another horror story, is it?"

- Politely stop the person and say something like, "Thanks, but I'd really rather not talk about this." Be honest about your nerves. You'll likely hear some reassurance instead. If the stories continue, excuse yourself to use the bathroom.

- Recruit your partner or a friend to be your advocate. Ask them to let people know you'd rather not hear about bad experiences. (This is useful at baby showers.)

- After hearing a horror story, debrief with a compassionate friend or your partner, or by writing about it.

- Seek out positive stories from people who you know had wonderful deliveries. In real life, the great births far outweigh the unhappy ones.

DID YOU KNOW that while some swelling of the face or ankles is to be expected, puffiness can also be a sign of *preeclampsia?* That's why you should pay attention to what seems normal for you, and report changes.

Visions of parenthood

*I had the distinct feeling throughout my pregnancy
that I was never alone. I always had company.*

DIANE LEWIS

Week 26

Baby Update

From here on out, your baby is gaining weight steadily in preparation for life outside the womb. Your baby is nearing the 2-pound (907.2 g) mark, averaging 13-1/2 inches (34.3 cm) long. If your baby is a boy, his testicles are starting to descend into his scrotum.

Body Update: Bed Rest?

Bed rest is prescribed for a range of reasons, including preeclampsia, placenta problems, carrying twins or higher-order multiples, and unexplained bleeding.

If your doctor suggests it for you, be sure to do the following:

- **First clarify exactly what is meant by bed rest for your case.** Can you get out of bed at all? Will you have to lie flat, or be in a semi-reclining position? Ask if you can shower, drive, walk up and down stairs, work, and so on.

- **Clarify how long you might be expected to stay in bed.** Until bleeding stops? Until you deliver? Will you be able to stay at home or will you be hospitalized?

- **Marshal a support network.** Enlist a point person, such as your partner, to help you set up the systems you'll need to work, run your household, or otherwise pass the time while you're on bed rest. Give some thought to what you'll do with this gift of time: Organize your photo albums? Write those overdue Christmas cards? Reread the complete works of Jane Austen?

- **Set up your "womb."** Whether it's at home or in a hospital room, create a soothing environment in which you can relax and feel as good as possible given your circumstances. There should be entertainment in the form of a TV with DVD player, laptop, books and magazines, and music. Add your favorite bed linens, pictures, and other pleasing objects to look at. Don't neglect fresh plants or flowers and other scents you enjoy, such as potpourri. Keep snacks and drinks stocked within easy reach. (Some women even add mini-refrigerators or coolers and a microwave.)

- **Find like-minded pregnant women.** One great resource: www.sidelines.org, the Web site of the Sidelines National Support Network for women on bed rest.

Mind Update: Choosing a Childbirth Class

Now is a good time to start looking into a childbirth class, which is best taken in the early to mid-last trimester. Sometimes classes fill up quickly, and you want to make sure you get a spot in a class scheduled to finish at least three weeks before your due date.

To find classes, ask trusted friends, your doctor or midwife, and nurses. Also consider classes offered at the hospital where you plan to give birth.

More tips for picking a class:

- Ask for a description of what the class will cover. Vaginal and cesarean births? (Most women don't know which they'll have; be prepared for either.) Drug-free and drug-assisted labor? Any postpartum recovery and newborn care information?

- Find out what kinds of relaxation and pain-management techniques are taught. Ask about the level of coach involvement.

- Read up or ask about the methods taught, such as Lamaze and Bradley. If you don't have a preference, you may like a class that introduces different ones.

- Ask about class size. You get more personal attention in a smaller class.

- Consider the schedule. An all-in-one-day course is convenient, but presents an awful lot of ground to absorb. A six-or-more week course requires a greater time commitment, but can aid retention.

- Consider the background and qualifications of potential class instructors. Personal fit is important, too. It helps if you "click" with your instructor.

DID YOU KNOW that "Lamaze" has become a generic term for childbirth class? There can be variations in what's taught in a given childbirth course, depending on the instructor.

What relaxes me

Childbirth class information

A new baby is like the beginning of all things—
wonder, hope, a dream of possibilities.

EDA J. LESHAN

Week 27

 ## Baby Update

Your baby is now about 14 inches (35.6 cm) long and weighs around 2 pounds (907 g), and is beginning to open and close his eyes around this time. The retina, which receives light information, is starting to function, and the brain is maturing and able to interpret this information. A baby can not only recognize light shining through your belly, but also turn his eyes toward it.

Your baby has probably adopted a consistent sleep/wake cycle, which may be the reverse of your own. (Your movements by day lull your baby to sleep. Many parents must teach their newborns the difference between night and day partly because of this.)

 ## Body Update: KEEP MOVING!

Reevaluate your exercise program to make sure it still suits your energy level, sense of balance, and comfort level.

If you're looking for some fresh ideas, try these:

- Hit the pool. Swimming is generally a safe activity during pregnancy (and it's great to feel weightless for a while).

- Try prenatal Pilates or yoga at home, as long as your doctor says it's okay.

- Join a prenatal exercise class approved by your doctor.

- Shop for baby furniture, put it together, and start decorating the nursery. This all takes energy.

- Clean house. Once the baby comes, household chores will likely fall to the bottom of your priority list, so take advantage and get organized now.

- Spend some time outdoors. Try taking a 30-minute walk every day.

- Alternate activity with rest.

Mind Update: CHOOSING YOUR BABY'S DOCTOR

It may seem early, but you'll want to have a doctor for your baby in place before you deliver, and the selection process can take a little time. First you'll need to decide if you prefer a pediatrician (a physician who has specialized in the care of babies and children) or a family doctor (a physician who could take care of your entire family, including your child as an adolescent).

Poll family, friends, and your obstetric care provider for recommendations. Ask about the doctor's sensitivity to different views, friendliness, and responsiveness to questions. It's also a good idea to check whether certain doctors are covered under your health insurance. Convenience to you (distance from your home and parking options) and after-hours availability (because children always seem to get sick at night and on weekends) are also important considerations.

Once you have a list of candidates, schedule some interview appointments to get to know the doctors better. Ideally you and your partner should both attend. Be aware that some doctors may charge for this visit.

Here are some topics to cover:

- Find out about availability: What are the doctor's hours? What happens if you have a question after hours? What about emergencies? Does the doctor have privileges at the nearest children's hospital? If the doctor is part of a group, can your baby always see the same doctor?

- Ask about how the doctor's office treats sick children. How soon can your child be seen if he gets sick? Are sick children kept waiting in a separate area?

- Discuss views on issues that are important to you, like support for breast-feeding or bottle-feeding, immunizations, and circumcision.

- Chat about the doctor's background and experience. Does he have any subspecialties? Does he have children of his own?

- Ask when the doctor would first see your baby and what would happen during the visit.

First impressions of the doctor, his office, and his staff count: Did you feel comfortable? Did you find it easy to talk to everyone and ask questions? Were the doctor's explanations clear and thorough? Were you kept waiting long before the appointment? Did the office seem clean and organized?

You'll be spending a lot of time (and money) with this professional in the coming years. Take your time to make a selection you feel good about.

DID YOU KNOW that shortness of breath is a side effect of pregnancy, because your lungs are slightly squished by your expanding uterus?

Notes for pediatrician, recommendations, impressions

Musings

I love being pregnant and feeling the kicks, rolls, and hiccups.
But I can't wait to see what our baby will look like.
Nine months is much too long to wait!

IRENE MANGAE

Your Third Trimester

(28 TO 41+ WEEKS)

The Homestretch

The last trimester of pregnancy is an especially exciting time of your life because You Are Definitely About to Have a Baby! You look it and feel it. Strangers can tell. The more frequent doctor visits say so, too.

It's a time of ready-to-go excitement and plodding fatigue. Of thinking about tiny baby clothes and barely being able to button your own. Of time passing maddeningly slowly and yet there not being enough time to get everything done.

Take advantage of these weeks to make final plans and preparations for motherhood. At work, make sure you've talked to your human resources contact about paperwork, insurance, and the like. You should also evaluate your post-birth work plans and plan your maternity leave or quit date with your supervisor. At home, you'll want to start assembling the furniture, gear, and clothing your baby will need, or, if this goes against cultural or religious conventions for you, at least make lots of lists of what you'll need, and make arrangements for their delivery later. With your partner, compare notes about feelings during these countdown weeks and share one another's expectations about baby care and finding time for your relationship after you become parents.

Think help, too! What do you need to know or do to prepare yourself for labor and delivery, for breast-feeding, for baby care? Whom can you turn to for advice? Where will you locate other new mothers with whom you can exchange ideas, complaints, and maybe babysitting, too? Network like crazy. Fire up the Internet to search for answers (and other women who share your due date). Call your doctor whenever you're in doubt about anything. And leave time to dream a little, too.

The last three months of pregnancy are a time for wondering, waiting, wishing, and—yes—waiting.

Third Trimester Dos and Don'ts

Do...

- Expect to gain about 1 to 1-1/2 pounds (454 to 680 g) a week this trimester. Your baby adds the most body weight now in preparation for life outside the womb.

- Eat lots of small meals. Your nutritional needs are the same as in mid-pregnancy, but, as your uterus compresses your stomach, you may feel more comfortable if you consume less at each sitting.

- Drink lots of water. Staying well-hydrated enhances blood production, wards off constipation, and may help you avoid premature contractions. Carry an athletic bottle around with you so you can sip all day.

- Continue taking your prenatal vitamins. Don't forget to refill your prescription before the bottle is empty.

- Keep moving. Exercise makes you feel better and helps your body to prepare, overall, for delivery.

- Rehearse your delivery. Know how to reach your partner at all times by the ninth month and have a backup plan for getting to the hospital. Take care of hospital-admittance paperwork ahead of time. And be sure you know directions to the place where you'll deliver and where to check in once you get there.

- Take a childbirth class that will end at least 3 weeks before your due date, so that you're sure to finish it.

- Continue doing kick counts to monitor your baby's well-being. (See page 98.) Pay attention to how the kicks seem to change as your pregnancy progresses. As space grows tight, they may feel less broad and more isolated and even sharp.

- Read up on breast-feeding and parenting techniques while you have the time. In the first busy weeks of parenthood you're likely to have less time.

Don't...

- **Be too impatient.** The weeks may seem to tick by slowly, but you should take advantage of this time to prepare yourself mentally and practically for parenthood. Also use these weeks to savor the relative freedom of childlessness and reinforce your relationship while it's "just the two of you" (if this is your first child).

- **Skip the seat belt because it's uncomfortable.** You're buckling up for two.

- **Overdo it.** Listen to your body, which may be signaling a need for increased rest as your pregnancy progresses. Aim for a balance between moving and relaxing.

- **Use step stools or ladders, or otherwise put yourself at risk for falls.** Your altered sense of balance is already a risk factor.

- **Ignore bothersome symptoms or hesitate to call and ask your doctor about anything.** (She's heard it all before, and is full of good advice.)

- **Pretend you're not pregnant.** It may sound hard to ignore the physical reality, but many women also try to deny the mental reality by avoiding talking about or thinking about the baby growing inside them. If this sounds familiar, explore what's behind this denial. Is it fear of how your life will change? Fear you won't be taken as seriously at work? Ambivalence about motherhood? There are no "bad" thoughts; the only thing that's bad is to ignore the reality of the unavoidable. Use your journal to write about your worries as well as your wishes.

- **Call yourself "fat."** You may feel that way given the extra weight you've accumulated, but rest assured anyone looking at you doesn't share this view. What they see is the miracle of a new life in progress.

When I listen to my body, it says . . .

Questions for my health professional

My pregnant body was big and scary—sort of
like James and the Giant Peach!

SUZANNE BEILENSON

Week 28

If your blood is Rh negative, you'll probably receive a shot of RhoGAM this week to prevent you from being sensitized if your baby's Rh positive blood mixes with yours.

Baby Update

During the second trimester the growth rate of an individual fetus began to vary somewhat based on genetics and other factors. By this week, the average baby measures a little over 14 inches (35.6 cm) and weighs around 2-1/4 pounds (1.02 kg). She continues to look fuller as fat tissue is added. The skin is still thin and a shiny pink, but begins to appear more opaque.

One thing you might notice more often now: fetal hiccups. They feel like repetitive blips, and happen more often now as your baby's respiratory system continues to develop.

Body Update: THE SKIN YOU'RE IN

The hormonal shifts of pregnancy can have some surprising effects on your skin. Not all women experience every change, depending on heredity, pigment, and other individual factors. Most of these skin changes revert back to normal after delivery.

Here are a few of the more disconcerting—but completely harmless—changes you may notice:

- A single thin, dark line stretching down your abdomen from the navel to the pubic bone. This is called the *linea nigra*. Believe it or not, this line was there even before you got pregnant, but it normally matches your skin shade. Though it fades after delivery, this can take several months.

- Patches of discolored skin. Called *chloasma*, this is an effect of your increased vulnerability to sun, especially on your face. The patches tend to look tan on Caucasian skin and lighter on darker skin. Take extra care to avoid overexposure and always use sunscreen when you go outdoors. (*Chloasma* can show up even when you stay inside, though.)

- Darker freckles or moles. Scars and birthmarks can darken, too. Again, blame hormones and sun exposure. Do monitor moles for any other changes, such as size or shape, and tell your doctor if you notice such changes.

- Very small outgrowths of skin under your arms or in other places on your body. Called *skin tags*, they're caused by skin rubbing against clothing. They often but not always disappear after childbirth. For those that persist and bother you, you can talk to a dermatologist about removal after delivery.

- Red, itchy palms and soles. *Palmar erythema* is a hormonal condition. Try added moisturizer made to calm irritated skin. Skin returns to normal after childbirth.

- Should you develop a rash (red, irritated, or bumpy patches of skin) tell your doctor. It may simply be the effect of dry skin or stretched skin being rubbed against clothing, for example, or a rash could signal an infection. Best to get it checked to receive the most appropriate care advice.

Mind Update: WHAT YOU CAN DO NOW TO AVOID POSTPARTUM DEPRESSION

Postpartum depression (PPD) isn't something any mother-to-be likes to think about—or thinks will happen to her. But in fact it's quite common, affecting up to 10 to 20 percent of new mothers, by some estimates. There are things you can do now, in pregnancy, to help protect yourself against it.

PPD is different from the so-called "baby blues" that affect the majority of new mothers within the first week or so of delivery. That kind of depression seems to go with the territory of shifting postpartum hormone levels, sleep deprivation, recovery, stress, and insecurity, and the anticlimax of pregnancy ending. Where baby blues and weepiness pass within a few days, postpartum depression is thought to be a different condition that is more persistent and can be difficult to shake without professional help.

A major risk factor for PPD is a history of depression. If this is something you've struggled with in the past, or have experienced during pregnancy, take extra care to address the issue now. Depression can also develop during pregnancy—some experts put the rate as high as 1 in 10 pregnant women. Confide in your doctor if you feel persistent blues, crying, or agitation; have trouble sleeping or eating or want to do either of these things all the time; feel worthless, hopeless, or suicidal. That's a broad range of symptoms, and many admittedly overlap some of the usual feelings of late pregnancy. But it's better to err on the side of caution and talk about your experiences; you'll feel better for it whether you actually have prenatal depression or not.

A strong support network after your baby arrives is a must. Start working now to line up as large a cross-section of potential helpers as you can—people who can help you with actual baby care or who will simply be available to check in on you and to offer encouragement and support. Work with your partner to put a postpartum care plan in place—don't assume you can handle it all on your own or that you're a less than "good" mother if you don't. *Every* new mother needs lots of help! Talk about how you will share childcare and what kind of resources you can tap into to offer added support in the early weeks, such as a meal-delivery service, a cleaning service, or hiring a postpartum doula. If paying for such services yourself is out of the question, consider asking for them as a gift when friends ask, "What do you need for your baby?" Babysitting co-ops, church groups, and the loving hands of friends pitching in together can all be helpful alternatives, so don't hesitate to tap into them. Odds are, excited well-wishers who care about you are standing by just waiting to be asked to help.

DID YOU KNOW that it's safe to get a flu shot in pregnancy? In fact, government health agencies recommend it for all pregnant women prior to flu season from November to March. (Note: If you are allergic to eggs, check with your doctor first.)

How I'm feeling

Ideas for my postpartum plan

You're braver than you believe, stronger than you seem,
and smarter than you think.

A. A. MILNE

Musings and photos

Week 29

 ## Baby Update

Your baby is now about 15 inches (38.1 cm) long and weighs around 2-3/4 pounds (1.25 kg). The head is getting bigger as the brain grows and develops. The skull remains flexible to enable the head—the largest part of the body—to squeeze through the birth canal, even though the rest of the skeleton begins to harden. It will remain slightly soft in places after birth. A newborn's head has soft spots that you can feel where the skull has not yet fused; they're called *fontanels*.

Your baby's senses are already up and functioning. He can see light and dark, receive sensations from touch, and the taste buds are even well-developed enough that the tastes of sweet and sour are discernible. Perhaps most exciting for you is your baby's hearing ability. Already he can hear your voice, music, and other sounds. A very loud noise will cause him to startle in the womb.

 ## Body Update: WHAT'S THAT ON YOUR LEG?

Varicose veins occur when there is a weakness in the veins that carry blood back to your heart from your lower body. Although this condition is often genetic, you can develop them during pregnancy as a result of hormones, the greater volume of blood being circulated, and the simple fact that there is more weight on your legs.

Varicose veins first look like tiny thin blue, red, or purple lines under your skin. They commonly appear on your legs, ankle, or vulva. You may also feel some pressure or pain in the affected area. They can grow to be thick, raised, or ropey lines and tend to worsen with subsequent pregnancies.

These tips can help prevent—or at least reduce—the appearance of varicose veins:

- Avoid standing or sitting for a long time.

- Raise your legs above hip level when you are sitting, when you can, and keep your legs uncrossed.

- Place a pillow under your legs when you sleep.

- Exercise daily.

- Avoid lifting anything heavy. Review a weight-training regimen with your doctor.

- Avoid tight pants, socks, and shoes. But do consider wearing light support hose, putting them on before you get out of bed.

- Try not to gain more weight than your doctor recommends.

- Mention the appearance of varicose veins at your next doctor's visit. In most cases they are harmless (except to your vanity) and, if you like, may be corrected after you deliver. Call your doctor if they begin to cause you severe pain.

Mind Update: GETTING READY FOR MOTHERHOOD

A good class on childbirth will help you through delivery—but then what? Use some of your last trimester to pave the way for your transition to motherhood. Knowledge is power, as they say—and it's also a great shortcut to confidence and a shot at better sleep.

Some mother prep ideas:

- Look into a breast-feeding class. It's a natural act but that doesn't mean it comes naturally to most women. A class can prepare you with techniques, tips, and other resources. Even if you aren't sure whether you will breast-feed, learning what's involved can help you decide.

- Consider taking a class on baby care. No amount of reading or even baby-sitting can prepare you fully for taking care of a little newborn. A class can give you a heads-up on the responsibilities involved and advice on how to handle challenges such as sleep and soothing. Many hospitals offer such classes, or ask your ob-gyn for recommendations.

- Talk with family and friends about their experiences as new parents. What surprised them most about the transition (in both a good way and a bad way)? What do they wish they had known then? Seek out those who have become new parents recently for the freshest perspectives.

- Read up on what to expect during your baby's first year, especially the first few months. You probably won't have time to read in depth then.

DID YOU KNOW that you can register a Web site domain name for your baby before he or she is born? If you've selected a baby name, try running it through a registry to see if anyone's picked it yet. Maybe your child will thank you later.

Role models and aspirations for me and for baby

My experience of pregnancy

Knowing that I was carrying another life was so wonderful. And the anticipation of wanting to get to know this new life made every ache and pain well worth it.

BETSY HORNICK

Week 30

Baby Update

We're up to 3 pounds (1.36 kg), 15-1/2 inches (39.4 cm), now. As more space is needed in your nearly stretched-to-the-limit uterus, several things happen. The uterus expands upward, shifting your center of gravity. (This contributes to the swayback posture characteristic of late pregnancy.) The amount of amniotic fluid in the sac also diminishes a bit to make more room for the baby.

The brain—which is one of the body's few organs that will not be fully developed at birth—is changing appearance as it develops. Originally, the surface was fairly smooth, but now distinctive ridges (the *gyri*) and grooves (the *sulci* and deeper fissures) form. These brain folds and wrinkles maximize its surface area within a small space. The brain does the majority of its "wiring up"—building connections between neurons that affect thinking and learning—in the first year after birth.

Body Update: STEADY ON YOUR FEET

That awkwardness you may be feeling is rooted in biology: extra weight to manage, loosened ligaments, and a scatterbrained quality that's the result of a preoccupied mind. So it's totally natural if you feel a little clumsy.

Here are some tips to keep bumps, falls, and spills to a minimum:

- Take your time getting around. Don't rush up or down steps and keep an eye out for obstacles in your way.

- Keep distractions to a minimum. Try not to multitask too much—talking on a cell while driving, for example, is even more risky now than usual.

- Wear supportive footwear. Even if high heels didn't bother you earlier, it's wise to lower their height now.

- Avoid unstable or risky positions. Standing on one leg, overextending to reach something, or using step stools and ladders should all be avoided.

- Do some exercise every day. Even light exercise and stretching can help you gain some balance.

- If you do fall in late pregnancy, it's a good idea to tell your doctor, even if you feel fine. She can make a quick check on your baby's well-being.

 Mind Update: READY FOR A BABYMOON?

Your honeymoon was a fun way to kick off your new life together. Why not a baby-moon—a romantic getaway, just the two of you—to mark the beginning of your new life as parents? Obviously there are three of you around this time, but travel, romance, and much deserved R&R will all be easier to swing before your baby's birth.

A babymoon offers a chance for the two of you to connect in a way that might have been hard to do in the recent months of focusing on baby plans. That extra strengthening can help to fortify you for the inevitable stresses that a newborn places on any relationship. What's more, you might also find that a short trip lets you forget your own worries and concerns about labor and new motherhood for a while.

Air travel is generally considered safe until late pregnancy, but it's a good idea to run your plans by your doctor. Many women don't like to travel too far from home in the unlikely event of an emergency or a premature delivery. But even a cozy B&B in the next town over can provide the kind of escape you need—and memories you will treasure.

DID YOU KNOW that you should discuss a postpartum birth-control plan with your doctor now? You can't know when you'll resume ovulation after giving birth. Don't assume you'll use the same method as you did before, as there may be more suitable options for your life postpartum. And don't assume that breast-feeding will "protect" you from conceiving.

What kind of dad I think he'll be

*I expected I would be walking around like they do in movies, all aglow, with
a drunken grin all the time, in constant awe of the miracle taking place within me.
Instead, for most of the pregnancy I just felt like a tired and hungry person
who had to buy new clothes every couple of months.*

RISA MAY

Week 31

Baby Update

Your baby is putting on weight more rapidly now—up to about 3-1/2 pounds (1.59 kg), or roughly half of the average birth weight! This gaining trend will last several weeks. Some of this weight is in the form of protective baby fat, which keeps body temperature warm after birth and makes the limbs noticeably plumper. Another consequence of this growth is that space becomes even more scarce, so your baby pulls the limbs closer to the torso in a curl that's known as the "fetal position."

Cool milestone: Around this time, your baby can start using little neck muscles to turn her head from one side to the other.

Body Update: COMFORT CARE FOR LATE-PREGNANCY ICKS

And now a few words about some less-than-jolly side effects of having a baby:

- Bleeding gums? Hormonal changes often cause swelling and inflammation, making gums easily irritated, especially when you brush your teeth. But don't put away your toothbrush. Instead, switch to a brush with softer bristles and use a gentler motion. But do continue to brush your gums as well as your teeth, and floss daily. These steps can help you avoid potentially dangerous infections.

- Sore bottom? Hemorrhoids, also called piles, occur when veins in your rectum become swollen (making them appear like piles or clusters). The increase in your blood volume during pregnancy makes you more susceptible. You may notice persistent pressure, pain, or itchiness, or sometimes see very slight bleeding. Always inform your doctor of these symptoms to rule out a more serious problem. To prevent and treat hemorrhoids, try relieving pressure from your veins by not standing or sitting in one place for too long. Do Kegels regularly and include a lot of fluids and high-fiber foods in your diet, which helps you avoid constipation. You may find relief at the site by applying witch hazel (Tucks) pads or taking warm sitz baths. Be careful to keep the area very clean. Never use laxatives or mineral oil to treat hemorrhoids.

- **Bad taste in your mouth?** Because your uterus is squeezing your stomach, its contents may back up into your esophagus, which you notice in your mouth. Smaller servings spread over more mini-meals during the day can do the trick. Drinking water also helps flush your system. It helps to avoid foods liable to irritate your stomach, such as anything fried, creamed, or sauced.

Mind Update: LOOK GOOD, FEEL GOOD

Nobody expects a mother-to-be to hide behind lackluster tents anymore. You can incorporate your pregnancy into your usual look whether that look tends toward Hollywood hipster, urban fashionista, workplace-practical, or athletic gear and Levis.

What's more, staying true to your style through the homestretch of pregnancy can have a direct effect on how you feel about yourself: positive, peaceful, beautiful, and (most of the time, anyway) vibrant.

Some universal pick-me-ups:

- **It's amazing how losing a half inch of hair here and there can make a woman feel peppier and lighter.** Or maybe it's the bliss of sitting back and letting someone else shampoo your scalp and man the blow-dryer. If you're leery of doing something as drastic as a major haircut, still make time for a regular trim to lose the split ends and restore a little bounce to your look. You lose less hair than normal during pregnancy, so odds are that yours is thicker and may need different or more frequent grooming.

- **Expand your wardrobe.** Yes, you're *almost* to the end, but that doesn't mean your maternity wardrobe should be closed to newcomers. Buy or borrow a few new items as pick-me-ups; remember, too, that you'll be able to continue wearing them for the first month postpartum at least. Many women swear by yoga pants or health care scrub pants (with elastic waist and a tie closure in front) for the final weeks of midsection expansion. Look for roomy tops that can double as nursing shirts, or a voluminous nightgown that will still look pretty even after delivery, when you're not filling out so much of the fabric.

- **Jazz up your accessories.** Feel like everyone keeps staring at your midsection when you're trying to carry on a conversation with them? New earrings or necklaces or a bright scarf will draw attention from your middle to your face.

- **Try meditation.** If it's not part of your routine now, consider taking 10 or 15 minutes a day to sit still and undisturbed and let your mind wander. Quiet the self-critical "judging" voice in your head, set aside the planning and worrying, and just breathe deeply and empty your thoughts. Many women report that daily meditation provides them with an inner calm and strength that shows on their faces!

- **Go shoe shopping.** Hey, it works when you're not pregnant, doesn't it? And now you may have a perfectly legitimate excuse, since the same hormone (relaxin) that helps widen your pelvis for delivery also works on the ligaments in your feet. Many women find that they need wider shoes or even a half size larger in the last trimester.

DID YOU KNOW that even though we can send a spacecraft to Pluto, we still don't have a surefire way to prevent stretch marks? They're caused by stretching skin. While soothing, moisturizers and vitamin E oil help mask their appearance only.

The kind of mother I want to be

Meditations

Growing a baby inside of me was the most exciting experience of my life.

Shawn Weintraub

Week 32

 Baby Update

Your baby has probably gained a half pound (227 g) in the last week alone, for a total of around 4 pounds (1.81 kg). The skin looks smoother and less red while growing and filling out. Along with storing some fat, he is also building up a good supply of protein, calcium, iron, and other nutrients.

 Body Update: EVERYTHING SWELL?

There's more than your growing baby to make you feel big. Excess fluid often accumulates in your tissues, so you may notice swelling in your feet or legs and/or your hands. Some swelling, or *edema*, is normal and many pregnant women experience it.

But persistent or marked swelling or the appearance of other symptoms, such as severe headaches or a surge in your weight gain, can signal a more dangerous problem: preeclampsia (toxemia, or pregnancy-induced hypertension). Preeclampsia is a syndrome of sudden increased swelling, high blood pressure, and protein in the urine that can be dangerous to mother and fetus. Your doctor or midwife will monitor you for its symptoms, but you should keep watch for them yourself. With timely care, preeclampsia usually can be managed until the baby can be safely delivered. Then the condition disappears.

To help handle ordinary swelling:

- Choose to sit rather than stand when you can. When you sit, elevate your feet above hip level whenever possible.

- Avoid crossing your legs.

- Rotate your ankle gently so your foot makes small circles when you're standing or sitting for a while.

- Lie down (on your left side) for a while a few times every day.

- Drink more fluids, not less, especially water.

- Try wearing support hose. Avoid tight socks and shoes, though.

- Call your doctor if the swelling occurs suddenly, if you experience other symptoms, or if you can't seem to reduce the swelling in 24 hours. Mention any swelling to your doctor at your next visit.

Mind Update: SHOWER POWER

Some women love being the center of attention at their baby shower. Others dread the very idea of having everybody cluck knowingly and warn them how much their life is about to change. Your feelings about baby showers are no indication of your fitness for motherhood. Resist the urge to duck out altogether. The fact that friends or family want to throw you a party means they love you and are excited for you. Let them!

If you're asked for input, be honest about your preferences. If you don't like silly games, for example, maybe your shower should lean more toward an elegant tea party.

If you're asked what you'd like, do a little research so you can come up with answers that really help you. Bring a friend who's a mother to a baby store to help you evaluate the dizzying array of options and make intelligent choices. Ask for items you'll need right away, such as a car seat, feeding system, nursing pillow, monitor, baby bathtub, and crib linens. If it's a large shower, include big-ticket choices on your wish list in case two or more friends want to pitch in on a single gift.

At the shower, ask someone to record who gave what, so you don't forget. One fun and valuable idea is to ask guests to share their favorite mothering tips in a notebook. This can be as valuable as anything you might unwrap.

Relax and have fun. It's your day. Then the next day start on those thank you notes!

DID YOU KNOW that if you don't consume enough calcium, your fetus will borrow from your stores, setting you up for an increased risk of osteoporosis later in life?

Don't forget, baby needs:

Think of stretch marks as pregnancy service stripes.

JOYCE ARMOR

Musings and photos

Week 33

Baby Update

Your baby is a little over 17 inches (43.2 cm) long and weighs around 4-1/2 pounds (2.04 kg), for another half-pound (227 g) gain in a single week. Her larger size doesn't allow for her previous acrobatic maneuvers—there's simply no room. Instead, movements now tend to consist mostly of nudges, kicks, or jabs.

Many babies already settle into a head down position, the ideal position for birth. Some, especially smaller babies, continue to rotate for a few weeks more.

Body Update: Night Moves

Many mothers-to-be report increased sleep difficulties in late pregnancy. Simply arranging your body comfortably can be a challenge. And then, no sooner have you drifted off when your bladder—which is being compressed by the expanding uterus—signals the need for you to get up again. Or your baby decides to start practicing for the Rockettes.

- **By day:** Be sure to walk or exercise so that when it's time to rest, your body feels ready to drift right to sleep. Fresh air—by going outdoors or opening windows in your home—helps.

- **At bedtime:** Try a small cup of warm milk or chamomile tea to help induce sleep. (Don't worry that it will make you get up to pee; you probably will anyway.) Avoid watching TV or exercising in the hour or so before bed—the idea is to wind down.

- **By night:** Continue sleeping on your left side. Make sure your room is not too warm; as you gain weight in the last trimester you are apt to feel warmer than usual. Lower the thermostat or remove heavy blankets.

And speaking of bed, then there's the matter of late-pregnancy sex. Rest assured that intercourse can't harm your baby, who's well-protected by the uterus, and orgasm won't trigger labor contractions in a healthy woman who's not yet ready to deliver. Getting into a comfortable position is the greater concern. A sense of humor and a willingness to experiment are useful now, as is patience. Remember that intimacy doesn't only mean intercourse. Many couples find oral sex, mutual masturbation, or simple petting and massage to be both erotic and satisfying.

Mind Update: REWARDS FOR A JOB WELL DONE

Every week of the last trimester marks an occasion for self-congratulation! Pick a day of the week (Sunday, Friday?) to pat yourself on the back, and treat yourself in some way each week on that day until you deliver.

Some ideas to try:

- **Plan a feel-good outing.** Enjoy a facial or pedicure, get a makeover at a salon or cosmetics counter, or schedule a special prenatal massage.

- **Splurge on a super-comfy throw.** Make it your special nap blanket for the extra sleep you're craving now. You can use it later too, to "sleep when the baby sleeps."

- **Do lunch.** Pick a different friend each week to catch up with over a leisurely meal. Order dessert!

- **Putter.** Spend some time on your favorite hobby or try your hand at something creative like painting your own pottery at a paint-your-own shop.

- **Take some time off.** Carve out some empty space in your calendar to just lounge: watch a DVD rental, read a book or magazine, surf the Web, or just listen to some music and let your mind wander.

Baby hopes

About my baby shower

You should never say anything to a woman that even remotely suggests that you think she's pregnant unless you can see an actual baby emerging from her at that moment.

DAVE BARRY

Week 34

A baby born prematurely now would have a very good chance of surviving without long-term complications.

 ## Baby Update

Your baby isn't ready for a formal debut: most measure just over 17 inches (43.2 cm) and weigh under 5 pounds (2.27 kg). But survival rates for preemies born at this stage are good, largely because the lungs are now more developed and in rehearsal for breathing outside the womb. Combined with the strengths of modern prenatal care, babies born too soon but who have made it this far can usually beat the odds and grow to live healthy normal lives.

The fingernails and toenails that are growing can be long enough at birth that you'll need to put little mittens and booties on your baby's hands and feet to prevent him from scratching himself.

 ## Body Update: An Easy Lift

The closer you get to your due date, the more inclined you may be, on some days, to just drop into the sofa and stay there until somebody wakes you to deliver. Your belly may feel heavy and cumbersome, your legs overworked, and the fatigue that disappeared after the early weeks of pregnancy is back. You would be ignoring your body's needs if you didn't just flop down and give yourself a break now and then. At the same time, you can't let yourself become a couch potato with child. Getting up and moving some every day helps to prepare your body for labor. Exercise also lifts mood and helps you ward off that slow "trapped" feeling.

Aim for easy exercises you can do all day long. Build in more breaks while working to stretch and take long, deep breaths. Sneak in a little walking by dropping off your mail at a mailbox some blocks away, parking farther from the entrance, or window shopping at the mall. If working out several times a week is no longer appealing, try every other day. Stop to rest and hydrate frequently. You may find swimming a good option now. The buoyancy you feel in the water can be just the relief you're looking for.

Mind Update: Your Birth Plan

A birth plan isn't a formal, binding document. It's not even a necessary thing to have. What drafting a simple, easy-to-read document outlining your preferences for labor and delivery does, however, is help you to think through your options ahead of time and to communicate your preferences later to the doctor and staff on hand during the birth.

The most effective birth plans are short—about a page—because too much detail is not likely to be remembered or sorted through in the heat of the moment. Besides, you can't control every aspect of your delivery no matter how careful and considered your ideal plan. There are too many variables and unknowns that might come up. That said, it's a great idea to have a general sense of the kind of birth you envision.

Ideally you'll have discussed these preferences with your doctor prenatally. A copy of your plan can be placed in your records as a kind of "top-line summary."

Think of creating a birth plan as your opportunity to turn your attention fully to the reality of labor and delivery. What do you prefer to try for pain relief? Whom do you want with you in the delivery room and after? What are your baby-care preferences immediately after delivery? For ideas of what kind of information to include, educate yourself about childbirth as much as you can, and look online for sample plans and guides. Gather input from other mothers, your doctor and childbirth educator, and a lactation or breast-feeding consultant.

Be sure to go over your plan with your doctor to make sure your desires are clear and your expectations are realistic. Know that hospital policies may affect how your labor is managed, so go over with your doctor areas where your preferences and standard care diverge. Your goal is to be as calm and confident in the delivery room as possible; you don't want to be haggling over practices then.

Some starting questions:

- What is your attitude toward induction? Episiotomy? IVs? Electronic fetal monitoring?

- Would you prefer to stay in one place or to move around during labor?

- What techniques would you like to try for managing pain? How do you feel about the various forms of medicated pain relief (epidural, intravenous medication)?

- What would you like to consume during labor (fluids, small snacks, etc.)?

- What position(s) would you like to try during the pushing stage (reclined, sitting, squatting, etc.)?
- When would you like the cord cut (immediately or after it stops pulsating) and whom would you like to do it? **Do you want to bank cord blood?**
- How do you prefer to feed your baby?
- If the baby is a boy, do you want him circumcised?

Once you finalize your plan, give a copy to your doctor and have a couple of copies ready to take with you to the hospital. Remember this document is not a binding contract. You can also discuss the variables with your doctor verbally. Make sure that your partner and/or labor supporter are on board with your preferences so he or she can be your ally while you're laboring.

DID YOU KNOW that your uterus expands to 500 times its normal size in pregnancy? (So that's why you feel so big!)

My vision for the birth

Third trimester thoughts

To speak of birth . . . to touch people's hearts and souls and to awaken that
part of humankind that has forgotten that it matters enormously
how a baby comes into the world . . . that is our task.

VICKI CHAN AND NIC EDMONDSTONE

Week 35

 ## Baby Update

Physical development is now almost done, but the "finishing touches"—most important, filling out with protective baby fat—are still underway. This week the average baby is about 18 inches (45.7 cm) long and weighs around 5-1/4 pounds (2.38 kg).

The liver is starting to function, processing waste. Your baby's liver needs to get ready to break down bilirubin, a byproduct of red blood cells. (If it can't do this effectively by the time your baby is born, bilirubin may accumulate in the blood and cause jaundice.) The kidneys are also well developed now. And your baby may be feeling some of your Braxton-Hicks contractions (see page 170), even if you haven't noticed them yet.

 ## Body Update: THE BREAST OF THE STORY

Your bump isn't the only part of your profile that's growing. As your due date nears, you may notice your breasts becoming larger and heavier. Your body is gearing up to nurse your baby. You may even notice a watery clear or yellowish fluid leaking from your nipples. This is colostrum, the "pre-milk" that's especially nutrient- and antibody-rich and will be replaced by regular breast milk (which looks more like cow's milk) a few days after your baby's birth.

This new cleavage might make you feel—and look—downright alluring. Make sure you're comfortable as well. You'll probably need to invest in a new bra or two for more room and adequate support. Check out a good nursing bra, which can serve double duty for now and for later. Look for one that's made of cotton (which is more breathable and doesn't require time-consuming hand washing), has wide nonelastic straps (for added support without irritation), opens in the front (for nursing—panels that separate are extra convenient), and has expandable cups with no underwire. To keep leaks from showing through your clothing, try disposable or washable breast pads made especially for nursing mothers.

NOTE: The test for Group B Streptococci (Group B strep, or GBS) is usually done via a swab of the vagina and rectum between 35 and 37 weeks. A common bacterium, GBS can be passed to a baby during birth, and is easily treated by giving the mother IV antibiotics during labor.

 Mind Update: WHOM DO YOU WANT AT YOUR DELIVERY?

A couple of generations ago, the only family member present at childbirth was the laboring mother herself. Even Dad was banished to a distant waiting room. Now he's not only expected to stay right at his partner's side, but grandparents, siblings, friends, and other relatives want to be there, too. You can even hire a professional labor coach (a doula) to provide experienced support in a way that your mate might not feel able to do.

How many people are too many? You can't really be sure until you're in labor. Some women invite a crowd to a "birth party," only to want to be left alone to their primal privacy as labor progresses. Others know they want to leave the sanctity of birth between themselves and their partner alone.

Just because you've seen a crowd gathered around a laboring woman on TV cajoling her to "Push! Push!" doesn't mean that this trend is what you should do yourself. It's your delivery, your choice. Don't succumb to pressure or hints from those who would like to join you.

Do consider hiring a doula if your partner feels uneasy about his ability to help you in the delivery room, if there's any chance your chosen labor coach might be traveling or otherwise unavailable when you go into labor, or if you simply think you'd like the extra help. Doula-assisted deliveries have been shown in some research to have shorter labors and fewer complications, possibly because the mothers experience less stress. Note that there are doulas who accompany the mother through labor and delivery, and doulas who provide postpartum care. (Some do both.)

DID YOU KNOW that in some European and Far Eastern countries, acupuncture is commonly used as a form of anesthesia in childbirth?

How my life will change

Thoughts about breast-feeding

There are three reasons for breast-feeding: the milk is always at the right temperature; it comes in attractive containers; and the cat can't get it.

IRENA CHALMERS

Week 36

 ## Baby Update

Your baby measures about 18-1/2 inches (47 cm) long and weighs around 6-1/4 pounds (2.83 kg). The layers of creamy vernix and soft lanugo are beginning to come off now as your baby gets ready for life outside the uterus. He swallows these substances with the amniotic fluid, and they become part of the meconium in the bowels. That's the tarry, sticky waste that makes up a newborn's first poops.

It's very likely your baby has settled in the head down, or *cephalic*, position for birth, so brace yourself for some mighty kicks to your ribs. He may also "drop" into position in your pelvis now. If his buttocks or feet sink into the pelvis instead, this is called a breech presentation. Your doctor will have a good idea at this point of how your baby lies.

 ## Body Update: BRAXTON-HICKS CONTRACTIONS

You've probably heard of Braxton-Hicks contractions, but you may not know exactly what they are or how to tell you're having them. These involuntary "practice" contractions occur when the muscles of your uterus (which will help push your baby during labor) tighten for 30 seconds to a few minutes and then relax. You may feel or see your abdomen harden, notice a strange squeeze or cramp, or simply sense some pressure. A key way that Braxton-Hicks contractions differ from true contractions is that they don't get longer or closer together over time.

Many women feel these contractions for days to weeks before true labor. In fact, you've probably had them awhile before you ever noticed them. Even though they are painless, they can be slightly uncomfortable. Use them as an opportunity to try out any relaxation techniques you've learned to use during labor. If the contractions become too uncomfortable, try changing position or moving around to reduce your discomfort; they'll almost always stop.

Mind Update: YOUR BREAST-FEEDING PLANS

Will you or won't you? How you feed your baby is a personal decision, but the argument for keeping an open mind and at least trying to nurse in the beginning is pretty compelling. Some women are physically unable to nurse, but this is a small minority; your doctor can offer advice if you've had breast surgery or another condition that you think might interfere with breast-feeding.

The American Academy of Pediatrics recommends breast-feeding for six months to a year because of the impressive and unmatchable health benefits it offers your baby. (Turns out it's good for you, too.) But you don't have to make a yearlong commitment right off the bat. Take it one day at a time. Every additional week that you can breast-feed gives your baby extra health advantages.

Why breast milk is good for a baby: Because it's literally made for your newborn, it provides an optimal combination of nutrients and a dose of antibodies every day. These protect against infection, illness (now and later in life), and allergies. Breast milk is easier to digest than formula, so your baby is less likely to get diarrhea or constipation. The skin-to-skin closeness of breast-feeding provides stimulation and bonding opportunity.

Why breast-feeding is good for you: In addition to the closeness you'll enjoy, women who breast-feed may lower their risk of breast, uterine, and ovarian cancer; osteoporosis; and urinary tract infections. There's also the convenience factor: no bottles to clean, mix, or tote. You can also pump milk so that someone else can offer the occasional bottle by day or night. And breast milk is free!

All that said, a learning curve for you and your baby (it's a team effort, after all) can be involved. With practice, it can become second nature for both of you. Read up a little on the subject now. Having someone who can troubleshoot for you—a friend who has breast-fed before, a lactation consultant, a nurse—is a big help in the first days.

DID YOU KNOW that most hospitals will make sure that you have a properly installed infant car seat before you can leave the hospital with your newborn?

My support system

I was surprised and touched by both the concern people showed,
helping carry items. . . and by the way strangers came
up and asked me how I was feeling.

JULIA WOODS

Musings and photos

Week 37

A baby born this week is no longer considered premature or preterm; you've entered the window of a full-term delivery.

Baby Update

Your baby-to-be's hair might be short and fuzzy or rather long—up to 2 inches (5 cm)—and silky soft. Some newborns look bald. This first 'do is not necessarily a look your baby will sport for life, however. Even hair texture and color can change, turning lighter or darker and/or curlier or straighter as it grows.

The irises in the eyes now display color, but it's not necessarily a permanent feature either. They won't lighten or turn bluer, although they often begin as blue and then over the first nine months of life outside the womb, turn to hazel, brown, or a darker blue. Eyes that are light brown at birth may turn dark brown.

Average size now: about 19 inches (48.3 cm) long and 6-1/2 pounds (2.9 kg).

Body Update: TRUE OR FALSE LABOR?

Wait! Was that it? Anticipating the contractions that confirm you're in labor when you have never experienced them isn't always easy.

Here are some tips to tell the difference between the start of true labor and a false alarm:

- **Time how long contractions last.** If the length of each one varies a lot and they don't get progressively longer over time, then it's probably false labor. True labor contractions start at around 30 seconds long each and get longer as labor progresses.

- **Time how far apart they occur.** The correct way to measure this is to note the starting time of one contraction and count how many minutes pass until the start of the next. (Don't count the time between the end of one and the start of another.) If the amount of time between contractions is widely inconsistent, then it's probably false labor. True labor contractions follow a pattern, with the time between getting progressively shorter.

- **Locate where you feel the squeeze.** If you feel the contractions in your lower abdomen and/or groin area only, you may be experiencing Braxton-Hicks contractions.

Generally, you'll feel true labor contractions higher up, and they'll start to affect your stomach and back as they get stronger and longer.

- **Change position and see if the contractions change.** If they ease up, then it's probably false labor. True labor contractions don't slow down, stop, or feel significantly better with a position change.

- **Might you guess wrong?** Sure. But remember that labor is almost always a lengthy process for a first delivery. It's not likely to "sneak up on you," giving you plenty of time to get to the hospital. In fact, many doctors believe that if you've had a normal pregnancy so far, it's better not to arrive too early at the hospital. Let your body do the work of early labor in the comfort of your own home.

Mind Update: COMMON LABOR FEARS

It's not unusual to feel at least a tiny bit apprehensive about what delivering your baby will be like. It's one of those human experiences that are almost impossible to fully understand and appreciate except by going through them.

Among the common worries of late pregnancy:

- **"What if I can't do it?"** Thoughts along these lines cross everybody's mind: How much will it hurt? Will I say or do something embarrassing? Will I not be able to breathe or push effectively? Realize that the fears are normal and real, because you're facing the unknown. Realize, too, that you won't be able to plan for or control everything that happens during this natural process. There's no single "right" way to give birth. Prepare yourself as best you can by reading, reviewing childbirth ed notes, or talking to other mothers who had positive birth experiences. And then let it go. Tell yourself that you're going to ride with the experience, trusting in your doctor, your body, and your baby to help you along.

- **"Will something go wrong with my baby?"** No matter how many tests or ultrasounds that have indicated all's well, no matter how many times you've heard the baby's strong heartbeat, it can be hard to shake concern for your baby's well-being until the delivery is over and your baby is pronounced perfect. Reassure yourself that the vast majority of newborns are indeed healthy. Even if you're at risk for a particular problem, the odds are in your favor. Confiding your fears to your doctor or genetic counselor can help, especially if they are intense.

- "What if I'm a terrible mother?!" Women of all kinds share this rarely spoken fear: those who had good mothers, those who had bad mothers, those who love kids and those who never had any interest in babies or babysat for a single minute of their lives. This type of fear is actually articulating the opposite: an intense desire to be a good mother. Simply having that intention goes a long way toward making it come true. Remember that babies start out small and grow one day at a time, giving you plenty of opportunity and practice to get up to snuff. You won't need to tackle toilet training, back talk, and how to ride a bicycle right off the bat. And kiss your image of Perfect Motherhood goodbye. There's no such thing. The best part of being a good mother is that you get to define it your own way, not according to anybody else's terms.

DID YOU KNOW that breast-fed babies have been shown to have higher IQs?

Am I ready?

My labor hopes

My labor fears

Toasters and flashlights come with more detailed instructions than new babies.

ANN DOUGLAS

Week 38

 ## Baby Update

Although actual statistics vary considerably, a standard-sized fetus now measures about 19-1/2 inches (49.6 cm) and weighs around 7 pounds (3.18 kg) at this point. Just how variable are birth weights? A healthy full-term newborn could be a 6-pound (2.72 kg) bantam or a hale 10-pounder (4.54 kg). Both of those would be considered within the normal range.

Most of your baby's lanugo and vernix that once covered the skin have vanished, and she continues to add weight even though she's considered "full term" and, in theory, good to go.

 ## Body Update: SIGNS LABOR IS NEARING

The calendar is telling you the big day is, in theory, any day now. Your body and mind provide you with clues, too. One early sign that labor is drawing near is that your baby "drops" into your pelvis. This is called *lightening*. You may feel pressure or dull pain there or in your upper thighs. You may even look like you're carrying your baby lower than before. Two other external signs are the loss of the mucus plug or your water breaking. The mucus plug seals the opening of your cervix and may become loose as your cervix dilates. When this happens, it looks like a thick bloody discharge or mucus clump. If your water breaks, you may see and feel a gush or a trickle of warm, clear fluid. Although this is a popular sign of impending labor in the movies, in reality it only happens as a first sign of labor about 10 percent of the time. (If it does happen, however, call your doctor.) If you've been having Braxton-Hicks contractions, you may notice that you're getting them more frequently. You may also experience soreness in your abdomen or lower back.

You may also feel a surge of energy and an incredible urge to clean up, get organized, and prepare your home for your baby. This instinct is called nesting. Go ahead and heed this primal call, as long as doing so doesn't stress or overwhelm you. Since you can't know when you'll go into labor, you don't want to squander all of your energy reserves "feathering your nest" on the night before you'll need them to give birth to your little chick.

Call your doctor if:

- Your water breaks or you are leaking any kind of fluid (even if you think it's just urine).

- You notice markedly decreased fetal activity.

- Your contractions are 5 to 7 minutes apart (unless your doctor advised you of a different timetable).

- You just have a strong feeling that you are in labor. Don't feel sheepish about your uncertainty: Trained professionals can quickly determine your labor status and set your mind at ease.

 ## Mind Update: ARE YOU PACKED?

Considering that 80 percent of women have their babies within 2 weeks on one side or the other of their due date, it's smart to get ready for your trip to the hospital now, if you haven't already.

Here are some things you should pack for yourself:

- ☐ Your health insurance card and your hospital preregistration forms
- ☐ A few copies of your birth plan
- ☐ Your childbirth notes (from books or class)
- ☐ Lip balm
- ☐ A pair of warm socks
- ☐ An object you plan to use as your focal point during labor
- ☐ Massage oil and massage tools (such as a tennis ball)
- ☐ Your "goody bag" of relaxation tools for labor
- ☐ A robe and a pair of slippers
- ☐ A nightgown you don't mind getting soiled (and a second one with a front opening if breast-feeding)
- ☐ Toiletries
- ☐ Eyeglasses if you wear them (you don't wear contacts in labor)
- ☐ A hair band or clip
- ☐ Five or more pairs of panties

- ☐ Maxi pads
- ☐ Two bras (nursing bras with front panels if you plan to breast-feed)
- ☐ Your baby book
- ☐ A breast-feeding guide (and/or any notes if you took a class)
- ☐ An outfit for going home (choose one that you wore midway through your pregnancy)
- ☐ Your pregnancy journal

Here are some things your coach or partner should pack:
- ☐ Snacks and drinks
- ☐ A camera and/or camcorder and battery charger
- ☐ A list of phone numbers and a cell phone, change, or a prepaid phone card
- ☐ Laptop to send updates and/or announcements
- ☐ Playing cards and magazines
- ☐ A portable music device
- ☐ Toiletries

Here are some things to pack for your baby:
- ☐ Some diapers
- ☐ A few newborn-sized outfits
- ☐ A cotton cap
- ☐ Some newborn mittens (to prevent sharp nails from scratching face)
- ☐ A receiving blanket
- ☐ A heavy blanket in case it's cold outside
- ☐ An infant car seat

DID YOU KNOW that a newborn's first cries are tearless?

What I'm thinking

Self-care measures

*I feel like one of the women from the Renaissance—
big, round, and very womanly.*

JOANN OLIVETO

Week 39

Baby Update

This week a typical fetus is now just shy of 20 inches (50.8 cm) long and 7-1/4 pounds (3.29 kg). In general, boys are born weighing slightly more than girls.

Nobody knows exactly what causes labor to begin, but one theory credits the fetus: It's thought that a hormone deep in the fetal hypothalamus (part of the brain) might set off a chain reaction of events that move from baby to mother, sending her into labor.

Body Update: LABOR RELAXATION

A body that's relaxed is better able to work *with* the force of contractions. The techniques you learned in childbirth education class help you relax in labor.

Practice some of these tactics now and they may come to you more naturally in the delivery room.

- Slow down your breathing, as if you were going to sleep. Make each inhale deep and full, and on each exhale, drop your shoulders and let the tension roll off.

- Close your eyes and imagine the work that your body is doing. During labor, think of each contraction as another big step toward meeting your baby. (You can practice this when you feel Braxton-Hicks contractions.)

- Ask your coach to give you a massage. A special massage tool or a regular tennis ball or rolling pin can also help soothe tensed muscles.

- Concentrate on a focal point. This could be external, such as an ultrasound print-out of your baby or a particular spot on the delivery room wallpaper, or internal, like the image of holding your baby. In labor, you'll do this for the duration of a contraction. Try practicing by doing so while counting to 30, then a few minutes later to 60, then 90. Bring all your attention to your chosen image and the numbers you're counting off.

- Turn on some music. Soothing sounds, soft classical music, or your favorite songs can help relax you or lift your spirits.

- Play a hypnosis tape if this is a technique that you have used during your pregnancy.

- Visualize a place where you feel comfortable, safe, and happy. Maybe it's a favorite vacation spot, your childhood home, or your bedroom. If you discuss this with your coach beforehand, he can help describe what you might "see."

- Take a warm bath or shower.

 ## Mind Update: FRIENDS AND RELATIVES

Your friends and family can be among your biggest cheering section. Yet you may also have discovered that your advancing pregnancy has brought some subtle changes to your relationships.

Sometimes motherhood can be a wedge. Friends who don't have children may be thrilled for you—but just can't relate to your plans, worries, and preoccupations right now. You no longer have focal points that are quite the same. Whether your friendship continues the way it once did depends on how much both of you want to salvage things. Some mothers-to-be find that they are simply too overwhelmed and tired to deal with it. Sometimes a heart-to-heart reveals that each of you is aware of the rift and wants to work hard to find common ground anyway.

Sometimes motherhood can draw people to you. Colleagues or neighbors who have children might be more likely to seek you out, for example. Relatives—especially grandparents-to-be—can even insert themselves into your life a little bit more than you might like. Again candor really helps. Think about what kind of interactions you really want and need with the people around you.

Knowing other new mothers can be a huge help and relief once your baby arrives. Increasingly you are apt to find that some of your new best friends are other mothers (or, eventually, the mothers of your child's friends). This only makes sense, since your priorities, concerns, and pastimes are liable to be so similar.

So if you don't know many mothers now, consider seeking them out. That nice neighbor down the street you used to see pushing a stroller may suddenly become somebody you want to know better, for example. Many towns offer support groups for new mothers; check local newspaper listings or the bulletin board at your ob-gyn or chosen pediatrician. Prenatal class "reunions" (get-togethers after you've all delivered) are another good way to connect with new moms; see if some of your former classmates might like to form a new mothers' group with you.

DID YOU KNOW that U.S. President Woodrow Wilson made Mother's Day official? He signed the order making it a national holiday back in 1914. In the U.K. and Ireland, Mothering Sunday is celebrated on the fourth Sunday of Lent.

Checking in with my body, mind, and feelings

Ready or not?

I was always really excited about the process and concept of being pregnant, but it has been very different from what I expected. From the first days of morning sickness to growing through various body shapes to now feeling both very drained and full of anticipation, it has been a process of needing to let go to some extent.

LAUREN ROSEN

Week 40

Note: Your due date should fall this week.

Baby Update

Average full-term newborn stats are as follows:

Weight: 7 pounds, 5 ounces (3.32 kg) (normal range is 6 to 10 pounds, or 2.72 to 4.54 kg)

Height: 20 inches (50.8 cm) (normal range is 18-1/2 to 21-1/2 inches, or 47 to 54.6 cm)

Head circumference: 13.8 inches (35 cm) (normal range is 13 to 14.6 inches, or 33 to 37 cm)

Tall parents tend to have tall children, and short parents tend to have short children. One fun way to guesstimate is the "mid-parent height" formula. Add each parent's height and then divide by 2. Add 2-1/2 inches (6.4 cm) to find the probable adult height of a boy. Or subtract 2-1/2 inches (6.4 cm) to find the probable adult height of a girl.

Body Update: EARLY LABOR

Early labor can last a long time, even eight or more hours. During early labor, you will begin to feel contractions at regular intervals, at first about 10 to 20 minutes apart and lasting around 30 seconds. (Some women are not even aware of the first part of early labor, especially if they've given birth before.)

Contractions may cause you some pain or just make you slightly uncomfortable. They will become more intense, but in this phase you can generally continue to talk and engage in other activities. Gradually contractions move closer together, to about 5 to 7 minutes apart, and longer, to about 40 to 60 seconds long. As you move from early labor to active labor, these contractions tend to demand more concentration from you.

It's generally a great idea, provided your water has not broken, to spend early labor at home. If you get to the hospital too early, you're apt to feel more stressed than relaxed, which works against your body's efforts. Besides, there's not much the medical staff can do for you until your labor is further along.

Some comfort advice for early labor:

- Time your contractions, both their length and how long it takes between them. (If it looks like it's taking a while for your contractions to evolve, though, just time them periodically or whenever they seem to be increasing in frequency or intensity.)

- Pace around your house; go outside.

- Put on some music and dance.

- Distract yourself with a video, a card game, or some other near effortless activity.

- Have a very light, protein-based snack (since you may not want—or be able to have—food later, and you don't know how long your labor will be). Drink plenty of fluids.

- Don't overexert. Save your energy for the later phases of labor.

QUICK REFERENCE:
The Stages of Labor

STAGE ONE: Labor itself.

Early labor (phase 1): Cervix thins (effaces) and dilates to about 3 cm. Most women can still move about and talk easily.

Active labor (phase 2): Cervix dilates to about 7 cm; contractions become longer and require greater concentration (or medication); when most people think of "labor," this is what they mean.

Transition (phase 3): Cervix dilates to its full 10 cm; contractions are long with several "peaks" and run together; this stage is intense but relatively brief.

STAGE TWO: Delivery of the baby (aka "pushing").

STAGE THREE: Delivery of the placenta.

Mind Update: PREOCCUPIED

Who can blame you for feeling a little stressed right now? When you're this great with child, it's hard to think about much else besides your pregnancy: When will your labor begin? How will you know? What will you do? What will it be like? What will your baby be like? What will *being a mother* be like?

These thoughts can manifest themselves in you in many ways. You may find that your mood swings are more rapid and severe than ever. You may feel anxious, fretful, or just plain tired. Other times you may feel calm, excited, and *ready*. Your relationship may feel strained, too—neither of you can exactly understand the unique stresses of the other, and at the same time you're each preoccupied by those stresses. Add to all this the fact that well-wishers seem to be calling and asking every hour how it's going and whether anything's "happening" yet.

Hard as it can be, look for ways to take your mind off waiting. Go see a matinee. Dig out your favorite absorbing novel and start rereading it. Do some yoga or meditation, since the whole point of these activities is to let go of all the thoughts crowding your brain. Have lunch with a friend who promises not to say one word about the baby for one full hour. It's not that you can forget you're pregnant, but by purposefully turning your attention elsewhere for a while, you can find some much needed relaxation.

DID YOU KNOW that it's not true that only firstborns are usually late? More than half of *all* babies are born after their projected due dates; 35 percent arrive before the due date and 5 percent hit D-day perfectly.

Musings and photos

Week 41+

Body Update: HANGING IN THERE

As you move past your due date, your doctor will monitor your baby carefully to make sure all's well. These tests can show whether the baby is still moving well in the uterus and whether there is sufficient amniotic fluid. Possible tools include the nonstress test, contraction stress test, biophysical profile, and ultrasound. Your own vital signs will also be watched.

Whether you're induced is a question that's based on your and your baby's perceived health, the perceived accuracy of your LMP and due dates, and whether there are signs of impending labor. It's not a decision to be made lightly so be sure that you understand the reasons an induction is recommended or not.

Each day you have to wait for an overdue baby can seem to accentuate any discomforts you've been feeling.

Feel better tips:

• Soothe an aching back with a massage or a hot water bottle.

• Sit up or stand after eating to avoid nausea or indigestion.

• Do pelvic tilts to alleviate back pain or pressure in your lower abdomen and groin area.

• Take warm showers or baths for an all-over refresher—and there's no rule you should only do so once a day.

• Get out and about. Going for a walk, especially outside, can help your body and lift your mood.

• Sleep in a semi-seated position, as in a recliner or propped up on a sofa.

Mind Update: "HAVE YOU TRIED...?"

You may be short on labor pains but there's one thing bound to be in plentiful supply as your due date comes and goes: tips and tricks from friends, loved ones, and perfect strangers for how to induce labor.

Most of these, alas, are old wives' tales. They're unproven, unfounded, and unlikely to work. As long as they're harmless, though, hearing them (and even trying them, if you're in the mood) can provide entertainment to pass these long last days.

So have you tried . . .

Eating spicy food? Walking with one foot on a curb and one foot in the street? Eating pizza, meat loaf, Chinese food, or pickles? A teaspoon of castor oil? Drinking Grandma's favorite tea brew? Having sex? (There's a smidgen of truth in that last one, since the oxytocin released during arousal and orgasm can trigger contractions in a woman who's ready to deliver—but there's no surefire cause and effect relationship between sex and labor.)

DID YOU KNOW that technically a baby is not "overdue" until two weeks after your due date? Most babies today, however, are delivered before they are officially "postdates."

Reflections on my journey through pregnancy

*Pregnancy is an incredible experience, one that will make you
part of a new community of mothers. But you'll do it,
as you do everything else, in your own special way.*

LYNN ROSEN

Your Labor and Delivery

Bring this journal to the hospital with you so that you can record what happened while the details are still very fresh in your mind. Your labor and delivery experience is not yours alone; it's also your child's birth story. If you don't have time to record a full description of the day's (and/or night's) events, take a few minutes to at least jot down some notes about the highlights. They will jog your memory so that you can go back and explore the big event in more depth and detail later, if you wish.

Research shows that women who spend time processing and sharing their labor stories—no matter how difficult or easy the experience—tend to have happier memories and feel more satisfied and proud of the event. Seek out people with whom you can share your story. Write and think about it. Turn it over in your head. Yes, it's that big a deal!

Your body does something truly amazing and wonderful in creating a new life. Celebrate that singular fact! Feel proud of yourself and your accomplishment, whether or not everything unfolded the way you hoped or wished. Less than half the population ever does what you did!

How and when I first thought I might be in labor:

How I got to the hospital:

What happened once I arrived:

Progress of labor (high points, results of labor checks, length of labor stages):

What helped most:

What didn't help or appeal to me:

What was hardest:

What was best:

How it was what I expected:

How it was not what I expected:

Meeting my baby:

Who was there:

First visitors:

How I feel now:

WELCOME TO THE WORLD

Baby Basics

Full name:

Date of birth:

Time of birth:

Vital statistics: (length, weight, head circumference)

Whom baby resembles:

Birth announcement wording:

ABOUT MY BIRTH STORY

*I remember leaving the hospital thinking, "Wait, are they going to let
me just walk off with him? I don't know beans about babies!
I don't have a license to do this." We're just amateurs.*

ANNE TYLER

Photos of Baby

About the Author

Paula Spencer Scott *(www.paulaspencerscott.com)* is a mother of four and the author of several books about women's health, family, pregnancy, and parenting, including *PARENTING Guide to Pregnancy and Childbirth*, and *Momfidence!: An Oreo Never Killed Anybody and Other Secrets of Happier Parenting*. A contributing editor of PARENTING, *Baby Talk*, and *Woman's Day* magazines, she lives in the San Francisco Bay area.

INDEX